THE TOURISM AREA LIFE CYCLE

Its Application to the Costa del Sol

Pamela L. Perez

THE TOURISM AREA LIFE CYCLE

Its Application to the Costa del Sol

Pamela L. Perez

COMMON GROUND RESEARCH NETWORKS 2018

First published in 2018
as part of the Tourism Studies Book Imprint
http://doi.org/10.18848/978-1-86335-114-0/CGP (Full Book)

Common Ground Research Networks
2001 South First Street, Suite 202
University of Illinois Research Park
Champaign, IL
61820

Library of Congress Cataloging-in-Publication Data

Names: Perez, Pamela L., author.
Title: The tourism area life cycle : its application to the Costa del Sol /
  Pamela L. Perez.
Other titles: Ciclo de vida de un area turistica. English
Description: Champaign, IL : Common Ground Research Networks, 2018. |
  Translation of: El ciclo de vida de un area turistica : aplicacion a la
  Costa del Sol | Includes bibliographical references.
Identifiers: LCCN 2018035540 (print) | LCCN 2018038511 (ebook) | ISBN
  9781863351140 (pdf) | ISBN 9781863351126 (hardback : alk. paper) | ISBN
  9781863351133 (pbk. : alk. paper)
Subjects: LCSH: Tourism--Environmental aspects--Spain--Costa del Sol. |
  Tourism--Spain--Costa del Sol--Management.
Classification: LCC G155.S6 (ebook) | LCC G155.S6 P47613 2018 (print) | DDC
  338.4/791468--dc23
LC record available at https://lccn.loc.gov/2018035540

Table of Contents

The Sub-Region of Marbella
The Sub-Region of Estepona
Final Considerations

Conclusions
New Findings and Conclusions
Subjective and Objective Aspects of the Golf Courses
The Concept of a Tourism Destination Cycle
Temporal Conclusions Regarding the Costa del Sol
Spatial Conclusions Regarding the Costa del Sol
The Ecological Future of the Costa del Sol

ACKNOWLEDGEMENTS

My acknowledgements consist of a series of appearances of personalities, who performed in a magical theatre of altruism throughout a period of my intellectual production, when I was in desperate need of guidance. They were solely united by a spirit of kindheartedness and assistance. These accomplished individuals so generously extended their guiding and brilliant minds to me and luminously applied them to my incipient project. I wish to extend to them my gratitude in the chronological order in which they appeared in the theater of my creation.

The spotlight of gratitude should first be shown on the appearance of Professor Dr. Alejandro López López, Professor of Political Science and Sociology, as well as a renowned European environmentalist, at the Universidad Complutense of Madrid. Professor López López plucked my work from anonymity and navigated me down the road to obtaining a doctorate awarded by said university. From that time to the present, we have forged a strong and enduring friendship, always with the awareness of what, perhaps, my academic fate would have been without his belief in me.

The second star in my theater of gratitude is one that has so painfully disappeared.

It is owed to the late Professor Dr. Derrick Danta, who passed away in an untimely accident, practicing his passion, mountain climbing. Dr. Danta was a geography professor at California State University, Northridge, when he began guiding me on my formulations of the Tourism Area Life Cycle (TALC), and it was at his suggestion that I apply it to the Costa del Sol. Dr. Danta continued to work with me, even as he rose from the position of professor to Chair of the Geography Department, and, ultimately, as well as most deservedly, to Dean of Social and Behavioral Sciences at said university. I remember him, with gratitude, for his tireless intellectual support and amazement at his always kind, patient, and generous spirit. Dr. Danta set me on the path to putting together ideas, just as he put together the paths to the tops of the mountains he so much loved to climb.

The curtain on my theater of gratitude rises, once again, to welcome the entrance of Professor Dr. Adrián Pérez-Boluda. Dr. Pérez-Boluda, at the time, was an Associate Professor of the Department of Modern and Classical Languages and Literatures at California State University, Northridge. It was then and there that he distinguished himself as a true friend by selflessly and tirelessly editing the draft of this book, first published in Spanish, by Common Ground España. As Dr. Adrián Pérez-Boluda has risen through said department ranks as a full professor, first to become its Spanish Section Head, and now, most recently, to be the Department Chair Person, we have sustained a supportive and enduring friendship, colored by my always bountiful gratitude towards him.

Also, yet certainly one of the first to make an appearance in my theatre of gratitude is Mr. Pedro Muñoz Luque, Chief of Comprehensive Sanitation Planning at Acosol S.A., the public water company which manages water usage in the Costa del Sol. He began, at the incipient initiation of this study, published in Spanish, to take the time and consideration to provide me with the most updated information of the condition of the water usage in the Costa del Sol. For this current English edition, Mr. Pedro Muñoz Luque once again shared with me his most current findings, facts and figures, in the form of verbal conversations, as well as by means of the charts and graphs found in this book. To him, I am forever grateful for giving me the opportunity to remain current on the subject of water and how it pertains to this study.

Finally, I must extend my gratitude to my family. I must thank my dearest daughter, Joanna, who accompanied me on so many of the necessary trips to Spain. Without her assistance, loving companionship, as well as strength of stewardship, this book might never have come about. Lastly, but most primarily, to my husband, Bill, the rock of my life, who, with his love for the game of golf, illuminated me on the sport, and its usage of water.

Introduction

This investigative study considers the destruction of the landscape and how this converges with the problems of the Mediterranean. As a tool for the comprehension of this disarticulation, the region of the Spanish Costa del Sol is the spatial centerpiece, to which the Tourism Area Life Cycle Theory (TALC), devised by Richard W. Butler, is applied. This theory first emerged in 1972, in a paper presented jointly, by this scientist and James E. Brougham, in a conference of the Canadian Research Association[1].

At the time this theory became public, in this initial context, it did not create much of a stir among tourism studies of the moment. However, since its incipient appearance in the theories of this type, its importance has grown, both as a prescriptive, as well as a descriptive model of the life of a tourism destination which may be in a situation of either transition or stagnation.

This may be affirmed, as this theory has been applied to such diverse spaces as Hawaii, Lancaster, Pennsylvania, the land of the Amish, even to the Australian Gold Coast, and Venice, to which a study of this latter case is included in this book. Until the present, though, this theory has never been applied to the Spanish Western Costa del Sol. Now, for the first time, this is precisely the goal of this study.

To this end, it is necessary to establish the framework of the geopolitical space of the Western Costa del Sol, in the following form: Eleven municipalities, including the coastal foothills, form the Western Costa del Sol. From East to West they are: Torremolinos, Benalmádena, Fuengirola, Mijas, Marbella, Ojén, Istán, Benahavís, Estepona, Caseres and Manilva.[2] (See Map I)

With the application of the TALC, here for the first time to this afore defined dimensions of the Costa del Sol, its natural and socioeconomical problems are determined. As previously mentioned, historically, studies have been made in a descriptive manner of other destinations, in order to find the stage in which these are found within their theoretical components. Prescriptively, a pragmatic analysis has been formulated with the purpose of diagnosing the present and the future of these models, with this form of approach. The intent and the methodology of this study's research do not differ from the methodology and intent of previous studies. For that reason, it can be affirmed that the use of the theory, in itself, is not a novelty, but instead, it is the spatial framework to which it is applied.

An approximation to the essence of the TALC, created by Richard W. Butler, also may reveal to the researcher that the theory, in of itself, is not a novel one. In a deeper analysis, it can be aptly said that this model has successfully applied the Hegelian dialectics to a tourism space. The difference lies in that, in this theory, more

---

[1] J.E. Brougham et al., "The Applicability of the Asymptotic to the Forcasting of Tourism Development," (Presentation at the Research Workshop, Travel Research Association, 4th Annual Conference, Quebec, July, 1972)

[2] Enrique N. Jurado, ¿Puede seguir creciendo la Costa del Sol? Indicdores de saturación de un destino turístico (Málaga: CEDEMA, 2003), 23

specific categories have been fulfilled in order to arrive at the final stage of that body of philosophical thought, the synthesis.

In the TALC, phases of development are applied to the space to be studied. It begins with the *exploration* phase. Then, that of *participation* follows it. The *development* stage follows, and finally the ultimately sought-after *consolidation* stage is attained. If pertinent measures are not taken for its maintenance, this stage could shift into that of *stagnation*. Depending, upon the measures taken, by the responsible parties, be it by the private, or public sector, the area may fall into that of *decline*, or find itself, conversely, in *rejuvenation*.

It can even be said that Butler has found the similarities of life and death of a living organism in a tourism destination. It is born, it lives, and it grows. It goes through aches and pains, which may end in decline and decadence, if it has suffered neglect, in its maladies. If a cure is found for its ills, the destination may be reborn and continue to flourish. This complete process is that of the phenomenon of dialectics, focused particularly and applied to a specific space, rather than to a thought form. It is life itself. The destination lives, this being the thesis. The destination dies, this being the antithesis. If the destination ends in decline, or if it rejuvenates, this is the synthesis.

In this way, it can be affirmed that, in general, the theory in itself is not novel. What is new is its application to a tourism destination. In the particular case of this study, the application of this previously constructed model does not represent something that has not been done previously. As has been mentioned earlier, the Tourism Area Life Cycle theory has been widely and successfully applied to diverse and multiple tourist destinations. What is different, in this case, is its application to the Spanish Costa del Sol.

It is broadly accepted, by tourism studies, to qualify the Costa del Sol as a mature tourism destination due to the quantity and quality of the tourism development, which this region has undergone. The author of this book proved this fact upon completing an exploratory study through this designated destination. Perhaps, the most impressive aspect of this area of Andalucía, which lies between Málaga and Cádiz, is its almost 100 functioning golf courses built there, christening it thus "La Costa del Golf."

It is possible to qualify these courses as artificial characteristics, alien to the natural Andalusian geographical surroundings. This may be said, as golf is an imported sport and the design of its installations is not a function of its natural space. Their appearances are largely the same everywhere in the world. Therefore, allowing the conclusion to be drawn that the Costa del Sol fits into the Stagnation Phase. This finding is maintained by Butler, who stipulates that a tourism area begins to slip into this category, when artificial features, which separate it from its natural environment, begin to appear.

The foreign vegetation, which appears in these courses, along with all the chemical additives that they require, underline, to an even greater extent, their lack of naturalness, with respect to the environment. However, the most outstanding artificial characteristic is their consumption of water. Their insatiable appetite for this exhaustible resource does not adjust to what the supply of the climate of the Costa del Sol offers, as this region is part of what is termed, "Dry Spain." The point has even been reached, where the coexistence of the water availability for the needs of consumption of the population, and those of the golf courses are incompatible. To this point, the very existence of the daily life, of the tourists seeking sea, sun, and sand, and that of the community itself has been put in peril.

As no theoretical model, adapts itself, absolutely to any reality, thus, this study has devised and introduced a new stage to the Tourism Area Life Cycle Theory. It has been denominated the "Pre-Stagnation Stage." This addition to the original theory has proved necessary, as currently, it is proven that during the summer seasons, there is no notorious, or notable excess of hotel beds. Also, though a mature destination, the Costa del Sol still remains fashionable. In order to fit more accurately into the simple "Stagnation Stage," these aforementioned characteristics would need to be present. Therefore here lies the possibility of creating a new category, which allows for the inclusion of the Costa del Sol.

With the creation of this new stage, a contribution is made to the already existing studies on the development of the Costa del Sol. Also, it serves as a case study input of the empirical validation of a theoretical proposal, which has proven to be pertinent in other cases, as will be analyzed ahead. The adapted approach has been to superimpose the TALC to Costa del Sol tourism experience on both a spatial and temporal level.

As to the spatial or geographic application of the TALC, the focus was placed on the utility of the comparative method based on different studies, which are documented in scientific literature. To this end, a parallel case study was drawn between the development of the Costa del Sol and Venice. While both Mediterranean destinations are mature, the difference lies in that Venice is a historical city and the Costa del Sol is a region. However, in spite of this difference, parallels were found in both spaces. This was accomplished through Russo's usage and application of his definition of the concept of the "Vicious Circle," which he coined and applied to Venice.

This study has witnessed a development of eight chapters: 1) The theory of Richard W. Butler is expounded; 2) The origins of the theory are revealed, or that is to say, what influenced Butler to arrive at his conclusions; 3) The Tourism Area Life Cycle Theory's applications in other geographical spaces are reviewed and debates are mentioned as to the validity of both its use in practical or theoretical situations; 4) The subject of sustainable tourism is studied, which without this conversation, the destruction of landscape and its resources taking place at this time would be inevitable; 5) With the intention of studying the validity of the TALC, with respect to its application to the spatial framework, a comparative study is performed between Venice, a Mediterranean tourism destination and the Costa del Sol; 6) The theory is applied to the temporal setting, as the history of tourism in the Costa del Sol is traced from its beginnings to the present. In this chapter, it is analyzed and proven that this tourism destination has completed all the phases of the Life Cycle Theory, and it is now, situated either in the rejuvenation or the decline stage, at this point, in time. 7) This study also explores this region's surrounding physical geography; and, 8) The cultural geography, which makes up the Costa del Sol is researched and defined. An inclusion of appendixes, bibliography, and, of course, the conclusions drawn from this exhaustive study appear at the end.

CHAPTER 1

The Tourism Area Life Cycle (TALC): The Conceptual Framework and an Approach to the Case of the Costa del Sol

The objective of this section is to outline the content of Richard W. Butler's Tourism Area Life Cycle theory (TALC) in order to apply it in this study to the Costa del Sol in Spain. For this purpose, the content of the theory will be presented, and a parallel analysis of this theory, as well as the case study will be performed.

INTRODUCTION

Tourism destinations are dynamic, and it can even be said that they are a spatial reflection of a temporal dialectics, as has been demonstrated. These dialectics should be understood, however, as those of an evolution and not of a revolution, as might be interpreted by the Marxist dialectics or its precursor, the Hegelian method. Thus, it may be affirmed that the evolution of a tourism destination is a product of various factors. On one hand, the tourists' increasingly sophisticated tastes vary, and on the other, the natural attractions, which caused the visitors' arrival to this destination, in the first place, may be substituted for other artificial ones.

The proven paradigm in this study when examining the golf courses, which have been imported from foreign cultures to the Andalusian Costa del Sol, not only prolong but also increase the traditional tourism seasonal entertainment possibilities, while enjoying what the tourist industry refers to, as the three "S's"—that is, the "sea, sun and sand"—so characteristic of a summer of classical Mediterranean tourism. It can even be hoped that these courses become as popular as the region's original attraction, which is already denominated with familiarity as "La Costa del Golf."

Although the concept of evolution of a tourism destination is applied, perhaps more correctly, to the Mediterranean geography, as proven by Walter Christaller[3], there are also authors who apply concepts, such as C. Stanfield (1978), who deals with the same general theory when referring to the development of Atlantic City, New Jersey, in the United States and discusses "the cycle of the tourism center"; also, Raymond Noronha, who suggested that "tourism develops in three stages":

1. The Discovery Phase.
2. The Local Response to the Initiative Phase.

---

[3] Christaller, W. 1953. "Eitrage zu einer Geographie de Fremdenverkenehr, Erdkunde, 9, (2): 1

3. Institutionalization[4]

Within Christaller's concept, it would also be fitting to define the idea that a typical tourist's type and quality vary according to each destination. It can even be affirmed that there has been little research done regarding the average tourist's characteristics. To this end, little has been revealed about their psychological motivations, as well as desires. However, it is interesting to note that when a tourist is in the place and at the time of his or her visit, rarely, when interviewed, would they recognize displeasure or dissatisfaction with the selected vacation space.

Following this investigative aspect, Cohen (1972) has established a tourism typology, which characterizes visitors as "institutionalized" or "non-institutionalized," "explorers," those that do not have a fixed destination, in another words, "loose cannons," "tourists organized 'en masse'," and, lastly, "mass individualized tourists."[5]

Meanwhile, S.C. Plog has suggested in his studies that the tourist's psychology may be characterized according to the tourism destination's stage of evolution. In one extreme, there is the alo-centrical group, which is attracted to spaces that are unknown and that are defined by an adventuresome personality. This group is followed by the "medium-centricals," which are more numerous than the alo-centricals. They are found in places which have already started to become more popular. These locales are more exploited by tourism and provide a greater supply of services. This area will finally yield to the psychocentric tourist type, which is less adventuresome and conforms to old fashioned and outmoded destinations. Plog foresees that the immediate number of visitors will not be reduced, however, the market potential will decrease in size, when having to compete with more modern and attractive tourist destinations (Plog 1972). Plog summarizes his theory with the following quote:

> "We can visualize a destination moving across a spectrum, however gradually or slowly, but far too often inexorably toward the potential of its own demise. Destination areas carry with them the potential seeds of their own destruction, as they allow themselves to become more commercialized and lose their qualities, which originally attracted tourists"[6]

Therefore, according to this author, a tourism destination contains, since its insemination, the seeds of its own destruction, if contrary measures are not adopted constantly for its rejuvenation in a market which is increasingly competitive. If this is not achieved, the stagnation, or even the decadence of the destination may occur. This represents the philosophical idea that the affirmation carries within it the implicit negation, or that is to say, the thesis leads to the antithesis.

The synthesis in the application of the TALC theory could be the decadence, as occurred in Atlantic City before gambling was introduced there. At this stage, it was an obsolete destination composed of decadent and unproductive beaches. The

---

[4] Noronha, R . 1976. Review of the Sociological Literature on Tourism. New York: World Bank

[5] Cohen E. 1972. "Toward a Sociology of International Tourism," Social Research 39 (1): 164-182.

[6] Plog, S.C. 1972. "Why Destination Areas Rise and Fall in Popularity," Unpublished paper presented in the Southern California Section, The Travel Research Association: .17

synthesis could also be exemplified with this same destination, among many others, which are abundant in world geography, where the city's rejuvenation occurs. The intent is to demonstrate this same premise in the Spanish Costa del Sol, where the importing of golf courses are an artificial addition to this Mediterranean space.

Also, later in this book, other examples will be explored of tourism destinations, where the evolutionary theory of the destination, and of the tourist's personality may be applied. However, it cannot go without saying that some scientists (such as the previously mentioned Cohen) are reluctant to accept a unilateral conceptual body of social change. In spite of these contradictions, there seems to be overwhelming proof that the tourism area's general pattern of evolution—in other words, the TALC theory—is consistent. There may exist quantitative variations, but the qualitative values do not vary *a grosso modo*, in the majority of cases, in which said theory, is applied.

In order to understand Butler's theory, the concept of a tourism destination theory must be placed in the economic dimension, as well as defined as a product of consumption, such as any other offered in the productive cycle. With that degree of acceptance, this consumer product traverses the same market stages as any other, but with certain subtle differences that define and qualify it as a tourism product.

That is to say, the destination becomes known; its acceptance grows slowly until a point of acceleration. Following this, the consumption of the place goes through a period of stabilization and then, finally, its decline and demise.

In other words, the visitors will come initially to an area in small numbers. This area will be limited because of lack of accessible means of transportation, amenities and knowledge of place. Upon installation of better creature comforts and product knowledge, the number of visitors will increase. With marketing strategies and greater publicity, as well as better tourist facilities, the area will grow rapidly, and it will have an increased market.

However, upon achieving the carrying capacity saturation level, there will be a decline in the number of visitors to the place. This carrying capacity is defined by the **relationship between the level of usage and its impact.** The variables, which determine this relationship, may be, on one hand, environmental, which are represented by scarcity of buildable land, drinking water quality or air pollution. They may be artificial or physical, such as transportation saturation, because of lack of access to the destination by land or by air. Deterioration or scarcity of hotel beds may also be included in this category.

Another variable could be of a social nature. It appears in spaces defined by large conglomerations, or because of resentment experienced by the local population. This exists in direct proportion with the decline of the tourism area's attraction and its relation to other choices. This is due to over-use and the impact caused by tourists' visits. Also, the real number of tourists that come to the place to spend their vacation declines.

Also, in the Costa del Sol, there are large conglomerations in the summer months. Certain resentment is already arising in this space, in particular population nuclei, both nationally, as well as regionally. This occurs not only because of the crowds of foreigners but, also, because of their use of the important water resources, with the extensive irrigation, of the well-established golf courses, designed, for the enjoyment of their wealthy users. These courses are an object of criticism, as they are for the use of the economically well-to-do minority class, be they domestic or foreign. In these spaces, there is a poor relationship between the impact created on the environment and the number and quality of the patrons who use these recreational places.

THE TALC STAGES

The body of the TALC (The Tourism Area Life Cycle) is divided in seven stages, which represent the developmental phases, in which the tourism destination is found, according to its state of spatial gestation, either due to the public or private sector at a determined time.

1. The Exploration Stage

In this first stage, the visitors are found both in Plog's alo-centrical group, as well as is Cohen's explorers. Thus, these tourists belong to the most adventuresome groups. They do not travel under the big tour operator's auspices, nor with travel agencies. They make their own plans for their trips and follow quite irregular visiting patterns. Also, without ignoring Christaller's model, these tourists can be expected to come from far-away places and, at the same time, they will be attracted to the destination's unique and different natural, as well as cultural qualities. At this stage, no type of structuralization will have been developed to promote tourism.

Therefore, only local services will be available to this incipient tourist population, and at this time, it is estimated that contact with the native population will be high. Contrary to damaging this market, it is an incentive, which satisfies these tourists' appetite and tastes. The area's physical fabric and social milieu remain relatively unaltered by this type of tourism, thus, creating a very small social and economic impact on the life of the permanent residents.

This state in the present is not applicable to the Costa del Sol, nor to the Mediterranean, in general. These destinations in the present are in the phase, which some scientists have added, as an additional stage to the TALC. This is considered the "maturity" stage. Though in its historical past, as will be revealed later in this book, they have gone through this stage of exploration. Specifically, the Costa del Sol went through this stage of development during the last half of the 19th Century. However, this stage is still found in Latin America and in the Canadian Arctic Circle. Tourists are attracted to these areas because of their historical-cultural constitution, as well as natural characteristics.

2. The "Participation" Stage

Following Butler's model, and continuing with the evolutionary process of the tourism destination, the "participation" stage follows, where some local residents begin to provide services essentially or even exclusively for the tourists. In this context, as in the previous stage, the contact between residents and tourists is high and may even increase for the residents who provide goods and services for this invading population. During this transition, an incipient publicity campaign may appear to create awareness about this location in the tourist market.

According to Butler, a basic and initial area market may also be defined for the visitors. Here, at the same time, it is noted that a specific tourism season emerges, and readjustments will have to be made to the patterns of social activity, at least, for the local population involved in this industry. Already, a glimpse may be had of some sort of organizational modality and a more systematic travel structure. Now, the official institutions responsible for these areas take the initial steps of setting up or improving transportation networks or other services for the travelers. This pattern is fundamentally exhibited in the Pacific or Caribbean Islands and to a lesser degree, although it has also been proven to exist, in some remote places of Western Europe and North America. Spain went through this period after the Civil War and before the tourism "boom" of the 60's.

3. The Development Stage

For Butler, upon the initiation of the "development" stage, a clearly developed tourism market is defined, due in great part to a publicity campaign formulated and directed to areas which generate tourism. With the evolution of this stage, the local participation and control from within will be considerably reduced. This will be appreciated especially in the hotel industry. The small establishments, in many cases, managed by local families, will disappear and will be substituted sometimes by more modern foreign hotel chains, but without as much character, though with the creature comforts, which appeal, to the ever more sophisticated tastes of this enlarged population.

Also, in this stage, specific marketing campaigns will take place directed towards certain natural and cultural attractions. In some cases, these areas of entertainment may be supplanted by artificial and imported products, as has happened with the golf courses in the Spanish Mediterranean. As a symbol of this era, the five-star Hotel Pez Espada was built in Torremolinos. Under these circumstances, there will be transformations in the physical space of the place and these changes will no longer necessarily rely upon the native population.

Public intervention at the provincial, regional and state levels will become necessary, as has prevailed, in the Spanish Costa del Sol, at the state level, with the creation of, the Ministry of Information and Tourism, and later, at the provincial level, the Provincial Tourist Board of Málaga. The local residents may feel overwhelmed by the tourist population. The latter is more numerous than the former during the high season and the changes felt in the space may cause conflicts and disagreements among them. The need to immigrate to other places will arise, in order to cover employment positions, which are being created, to attend to the growing needs of this industry's dramatic growth. To this point, later in this book, a study will be made of the population settlements found within the urban areas of the Costa del Sol, which welcome the construction and service workers for its growing tourism industry.

Establishments never used before the transition, such as laundromats, will be found, in these societies.

Returning to Plog's or Cohen's classifications, Butler does not want to neglect mentioning that the tourist type will have been modified. For Plog, the medium-centrical type will prevail, and for Cohen, it will be the institutionalized tourist that will exist. The quality of their adventuresome personality is entirely lost.

4. The Consolidation Stage

As the moment of "consolidation" is approached, the visitors' growth rate diminishes, although, the total numbers still increase and the number of tourists, in totality, exceeds the local residents' corresponding numbers. The greater part of the area's economy has ties with the tourism industry. Marketing strategies are strengthened by means of extensive publicity campaigns for the purpose of extending the tourist season and maximizing the knowledge of the place. The industry's large chains and franchises' positions are secured in the area, but there are few additions other additions to this context.

The influence of so many visitors and services, which are provided for them inevitably will be the cause of much discontent and opposition among the local residents. This dissent is especially found among the natives who neither depend on, participate in, or benefit from, the industry's profits especially if their activities and their *modus vivendi* is found to be limited by this imported presence. This tendency is to be seen, in the areas of the Caribbean or in the northern coast of the Mediterranean. These regions' tourist cities have very clearly delimited entertainment commercial districts. Those less modern are considered to be second class and not as desirable. In this situation, the Provincial Tourism Board of Málaga developed the slogan, "A smile to tourism!," in recognition of the negative attitude, which was felt by the residents toward the invading population.

5. Stagnation Stage

Continuing with Richard Butler's established theory, upon entering the stagnation stage, the maximum number of visitors has been achieved. The carrying capacity limits for many variables of environmental, social and economic problems leading to such a situation have been reached or exceeded. The area has an established image, but it is no longer as fashionable.

The region depends on repeating visits and conferences, as well as conventions, in order to maintain the income level achieved in the previous stage. There is an excess supply of beds available and more efforts are needed to maintain a level of arriving tourists comparable to the "consolidation" phase.

The genuine and natural attractions are substituted by imported services. The tourist area destination is separated from its geographical atmosphere. There is new development on the periphery of where the original tourism exploitation once was. The existing properties change ownership frequently. This place typically receives the organized massified type of tourists categorized by Cohen, or the psychocentrical sort, classified by Plog.

The intention of this book is to demonstrate that the Costa del Sol as a mature destination is located between the "pre-stagnation stage," created for the purpose of this study and that of the "stagnation stage." Thus, a new phase is created within the tourism cycle. This is determined because, though a mature destination, it continues to be fashionable. Also, the genuine and natural attractions of the place have been supplanted by imported services, such as golf courses. These courses are developed in the periphery where the tourist activity previously was, and still is located, that is, in the coastal urban centers. Also, it is a mature destination, which still continues to be fashionable.

With these sports facilities, the forms of land ownership have been altered, as in their majority, farms existed in theses spaces before, where potatoes, peppers and other agricultural products had been cultivated. Also, the Costa del Sol is about to exhaust its resources, such as of water, due in large extent, to the demand the golf courses place upon this supply. This destination is not fully established in the stagnation stage because in the high seasons, there is still no excess of beds.

6. The Decline Stage

Following this scientist's theory, the decline stage comes next. In this stage, the area will be unable to compete with new localities, therefore, there will be a reduction at its spatial level, as well as with regard, to the number of tourists. It will no longer have the attraction for the extended type of tourism, but rather, it will attract short seasonal visitors, that is, for a weekend, or even, a one day stay, if it has access for numerous groups of people. It may also be noted that, the properties originally destined for the purposes of tourism will now begin to be converted to uses unrelated to this industry. As will be explored later, some scientists affirm that the moment of decline is approached when the visiting time span is shortened. However, it is not known as in the case of "the chicken and the egg," whether the decadence causes the shortening of the visits or *vice versa*.

This case, presents itself in Miami (Florida, United States). Here the hotels are converted into rest homes, apartments or rooming houses for retirees. Its physical attractions, as well as its climate make the place attractive for permanent settlement especially for senior citizens who come from this country's northeastern coast.

At this point, the place's resident population's participation in the tourism industry increases, as occurs in the cycle's first two stages. This phenomenon takes place because the real estate property prices fall in the same downward direction as the welcoming given by the tourists to the destination.

7. The Rejuvenation Stage

For Butler, the fate of the area's development still maintains its capacity for salvation, if instead of entering the decline stage, it goes into the rejuvenation stage. It is necessary to note that this reversal can only be accomplished, if there is a complete change of the basis, of the tourism identity's attraction.

There are two marked examples of this rejuvenation. First, there is that of the previously mentioned Atlantic City. This city was saved from decline through the addition and construction of casinos, in order to complement and bolster, the already decaying summer beach environment. With these casinos, the tourism stage is prolonged, both qualitatively and quantitatively. Thus, tourism has grown numerically, and the visits of these groups are prolonged throughout the year. Of course, this effect will only take place if there are no nearby places, which could compete with similar supplies of this product.

This case is also found in Europe with the establishment of spas, which cause the same effect in the tourism destination, as those in Atlantic City. Though the use and enjoyment of these rest and relaxation centers, with spring water treatments, have existed historically in this continent, and in the present, are commanding a surge of popularity. In the Spanish Costa del Sol, there are at least half a dozen clinics and hotels that offer varied services, such as hydrotherapies, seaweed treatments, talassotherapies and revitalizing treatments, which are open all year long, though their supply and demand are still small. Unfortunately, there are no natural spas, in the region. These are located in the interior, in Carratraca, and Tolox and are found slightly outside the surrounding tourist area.

Continuing with the intention of diversifying and varying the Costa del Sol's image of sea, sun and sand, there are also casinos. This region has two of the twenty-two such entities, which exist in the nation. They are of the best in the country. Torrequebrada (1979), in Benalmádena and Casino Marbella (1978) receive national, as well as international clientele, with those of high spending power. These casinos are located in five and four-star hotels respectively. They receive more that 300,000 visitors annually, thus contributing very beneficially to the region's economy.

Given the Costa del Sol's benign winter climate, the golf course construction prolongs tourism during this season and these months. Therefore, spring, autumn and winter are the high seasons for golf, as well as the classical summertime season, when the sea, sun and sand are also being enjoyed. A higher quality and quantity of tourism has been sought with the implementation of these golf courses.

Some Europeans who have come in the past, only during the summer market, have redirected their efforts towards the window of winter tourism. In this way, the location has experienced the benefit of a tourism market which lasts all year round also.

The development of new services becomes an economically feasible goal, as this market increases, and, at the same time, it serves to revitalize the summer services, which were becoming outdated. According to this theory, with these new product forms, it is even possible to have new tourism areas appear, which had not been envisioned previously.

According to Butler, in this dimension of a possible rejuvenation, it is very probable that both private and public stimuli, as well as efforts will be needed for the rebirth of these areas to take place. In this market it can be expected that the alo-centrical tourist (to use Plog's, already cited, terminology) will no longer come to this location. The arrival of the latter type of tourist is only given at the recommencement of a completely new developmental cycle. Although the tourist's motivations for visiting a specific place are not well understood, the norm is that this type of visitor is planning to enjoy one or more pastimes or activities, there.

However, it can be foreseen that this space does not have a permanent attraction, which might enable it to withstand the competition and pressures of other spaces in the area. Only in the case of truly unique places, such as Niagara Falls, can a consistency and constancy of human tastes and appeal be applied. Disneyland and Disney World may also be given as other examples of destinations, within the North American continent, which can retain limitlessly, and throughout time, the interest of the tourism masses.

As will be explored later in this book, it is even believed that destinations, such as these previously mentioned, will not allow for their own decline. They will go into a phase of redirection. By having such an artificial base, these mega constructions can combat the effects of loss of interest, with the passage of time, simply by building new attractions. Many loyal visitors remain attracted to these constantly rejuvenated places, nor do their preferences for theses destinations palpably change for many years to come.

However, it must be added that these tourism preferences are maintained, as a function of price and accessibility, more than because of tastes and predispositions. Marx's economic determinism comes into play here. It may also be concluded that tourists of the pychocentrical type, defined by Plog, in his tourism theory, come to this destination.

Butler cautiously affirms that it is important to emphasize that not all tourism destinations adjust, in such a clear manner, to this conceptual model of the tourism areas' evolution. In the Mexican city of Cancun, in its product study, it may be argued that when developing, it entirely omitted the exploration, and participation phases.

At the least, it can be said that these phases had a minimal impact on its economic development, upon becoming a tourism destination of instant consumption. This happens with the era of computerized selection, which allows for a range of possibilities permitted by certain prefixed parameters. In the case of Cancun, it can be concluded that the product takes off in the development phase, even though, it can be argued that all of Mexico, on a national scale, and in its entirety, experiments the complete cycle. The latter can be sustained, as no tourism destination can begin in a total vacuum. Everything has to have its seeds of initiation and its process of recognition represents a domino effect in geometric progression.

TOWARD A FIRST APPROACH TO THE APPLICATION OF THE LIFE CYCLE THEORY OF THE TOURIST AREAS OF THE COSTA DEL SOL

The dangerous presumption that tourism destinations are attractive and that they will always be that way is implicit in the incipient planning of this economic product.

This latent generalization, which is a given, is found reflected in the public policy, and of the private sector's *laissez-faire* behavior. It is also reflected in the *quasi*-anarchical population growth and in the installations, as well as the infrastructures, which occurred in the 70's, 80's and 90's, in the Andalusian Costa del Sol. This is proven by the current saturation of the region's future, as well as present carrying capacity. Only very recently has any consideration been given to its possible demise in the tourism market.

This is due, in general, to the fact that the tourism industry has proven to have an almost inexhaustible capacity for growth. The case of the Costa del Sol does not differ from this rule.

As indicated by Juradao Arrones, the tourism affluence from 1965 to 1975, according to the *Western Costa del Sol Planification Scheme,* took off quantitatively between 1961-63, with foreign demand (77% of total arrivals), especially composed of Germans, British, Americans, Dutch and French. Jurado highlights the importance of the American market, not so much because of its quantity, but because of its high purchasing power.

More revealing information underlines the evolution of overnight stays in official lodgings as a reflection of the explosive process, which characterizes this stage. The Costa del Sol overnight stays went from five million in 1968 to 18 million in 1972. It experienced an increase of an average stay of 5.7 days[7] in 1968, to 8.4 days in 1972, while Spain, in its entirety, had an estimate stay of 5.9 in 1971.

However, the two energy crises (the first, in 1973, and the second, in 1979) created inflationary situations, in the countries of demand, causing a scarcity of money, which was normally destined to planning for vacations.

These increases of prices, which affected the demand, also had negative repercussions on the supply. This created a deficit in construction and on the capacity to maintain an abundant workforce supply. The situation leads to the abandonment of tourism projects. Those already completed gave the space an appearance of deterioration and degeneration. At the beginning of the 90's, there was also another crisis. This, however, was not of an economical type but one of political nature, which occurred, due to, the military crisis in the Persian Gulf (or the so called, Gulf War).

In spite of these ups and downs in the tourism demand, the public authorities and the private sector preferred to continue with the unbridled structural construction and expansion. The globalized mentality was one of the tourism industry being the hen that laid golden eggs. What is considered to be the basic fact of the tourist industry is that the massive wave of tourists who arrive to enjoy the three S's in the Spanish Costa del Sol will increase, *ad infinitum,* without the loss of its enchantment and attraction. This presumption's fallacy is found in this specific space's history, as well as, in that of other mature tourism destinations.

On the other hand, according to Butler's theory, upon reaching the level of carrying capacity, if the number of visitors is increased, or if the location matures, it is understood that the destination will lose the elements that make it attractive. Within this loss, a change in the attitude towards tourism, on the part of the local residents may be included. This change, in the reception to the tourism population can be found in the process suggested by Doxey in his "irredex" theory, which means the index of irritation towards the tourist. This is a progressive scale, which begins with euphoria,

---

[7] Jurdao Arrones, F., 1990. *España en venta.* Madrid: Ediciones Endión, 1990

continues into a state of apathy, or irritability and, in some cases, arrives at a condition of antagonism.[8]

However, Butler finds this theory a little outmoded, even though, it is still of interest to him. The most recent research has proven that the reaction of local residents to tourism is not necessarily due to increase in contact between visitor and host or the increase in the number of tourists.

For Butler, the causality is found, rather as a more complex function, of the relationship between host and visitor and the involved area's specific ordering.

The Costa del Sol has reached this index of antagonism between some nuclei of the native population given the extended establishment of golf courses in the Costa del Sol. To this point, the region has already been denominated the Costa del Golf, because of its inefficient use of these scarce and exhaustible resources, such as water.

If the TALC theory is applied to a tourism space, after a period of stabilization, a range of developmental situations can be expected. The previously mentioned case of Atlantic City may be given, which reflects a more prosperous situation. The economy becomes enlarged and growth is renewed, with the new direction, this place's tourism attraction has taken. The Costa del Sol could grow, with only a few minor modifications. Such radical renovations are unnecessary. Carrying capacity readjustments and continued resource protection might permit the continuation of the region's growth, albeit, to a lesser degree, than in the case of Atlantic City. Though the Costa del Sol's economy has widened with the introduction of golf, and with care of its natural resources, it could continue to do so.

For Butler, if the level of visitors falls absolutely, initially readjustments will have to be made to all capacity levels, thus, ensuring the maintenance of a more stable level of affluence. If there continues to be a resource overload, without its care and renovation, added to a decline in competivity with other resources, in other destinations, there will also be a marked decline in visitors. If the Costa del Sol's aquifer resources do not receive the required conservation treatment, they could also meet their decline.

Finally, according to Butler's theory, the worst thing for the health of tourism destination is the intervention of war, epidemics or other catastrophic events. These can result in an immediate decline in the number of tourist arrivals. This military event was already mentioned before when touching upon, the negative effects on the product due to the Gulf War. These situations can make it difficult to reestablish the area as an attractive destination. It may even lose its appeal completely even when the problem has been resolved. This situation, as will be analyzed later in this book, occurred during the Spanish Civil War.

In order to demonstrate Butler's hypothesis, it is very necessary to have quantifiable figures of the tourism destination's last thirty or forty years, that is to say, for a prolonged temporal period. Fortunately, the Costa del Sol is a mature tourism destination and has this industry's numerical information for the past forty years, that is to say, since the 60's.

---

[8] Doxey, G.V., 1975 " A Causation Theory of Visitor---Resident Irritants: Methodology and Research Inferences," *Proceedings of the Travel Research Association Sixth Annual Conference Travel Research Association:* 195

At the same time, the developmental stage of different spaces varies according to factors, such as its rate of development, its number of visitors, the accessibility to its space, the policy of the prevailing governments towards it and the number of similar areas which compete with similar attraction resources.

This last case has occurred in the Costa del Sol, with the extension and improvement of air, as well as ground transportation. In terms of aviation communications, the Málaga airport was enlarged in 1961. This event was accompanied by a price reduction in commercial flights arriving to the city, as well as the sale of vacation packages by big international tour operators. In this way, an increase of visitors arriving to the region was felt.

Historically, in the region, the power of horses' and mules' muscles, were substituted, by the railroad, during the decade of the '60's, in the 19th century. In more recent history, the N-340 highway is the region's principal artery of ground transportation. It took longer to materialize, than the airport but, once established, it has served as the backbone for tourism settlements and a distributor of tourist nuclei who arrive by air to the province. It is also responsible for the spatial location of many of the golf courses and their respective residential developments. With the construction of the AVE (high speed) train it will take only a few hours to arrive in Málaga from Madrid.

According to Butler, if the development of services or its accessibility is delayed, for any reason, whether it be for lack of capital, lack of outside interest or local opposition, the exploration period may be much longer than anticipated. In the places of "instant destinations," where there has been little or no previous settlement, the initial exploration and participation stages in the place may be insignificant or very shortened. Noronha notes this situation to be applicable, in under developed or developing countries.

Butler has analyzed that the classical tourism destinations, such as the Costa del Sol, and in general, those of the northern Mediterranean, Great Britain, the northeastern United States and many parts of Florida, in this country's South East, have passed, with certainty, through all the evolutionary stages of this process. Other areas, such as Hawaii, the islands of the Pacific, those of the Caribbean and some destinations of North Africa, still have not overcome all the developmental stages. They may be found, rather, in the post-consolidation phase, at this time, in the 21st century.

This cycle, described by Richard Butler, suggests that a change of focus is required regarding the tourism destination's life. This responsibility for the transformation of the treatment of these spaces falls upon those that plan, develop and manage these areas. The tourism attractions should not be seen as goods, which are inexhaustible, or atemporal. They must be valued as a finite economic product and one, which is, possibly, non-renewable.

THE FINITUDE OF DESTINATIONS AND THE COSTA DEL SOL

With Butler's vision, the destinations could be better protected and preserved. The tourism area's development could be maintained within the limits of a predetermined capacity and its competitively in the potential market could be preserved during a more prolonged period. Definitely, with this philosophy, a situation could be achieved where the maximum number of people who visit a place might be less than what is found in the present system of development, especially, over the short term. In this way, more assistance could be given to visitors over the long term. The policy, which is practiced, today, in locations such as the Costa del Sol, is that of, feast for today, but famine for tomorrow.

This policy is trying, to be achieved, in the Costa del Sol, with the intention of prolonging, the vacation period, throughout the year, with the incentive of greater attractions at many levels. The extensive introduction of golf courses in the region is an example of this. The ability to practice this sport, on a year-long basis, also extends the vacation period during this time span.

Within the sporting framework, a commitment to the equestrian sports, with its consequent racetracks, is also made. In this setting, the strategy is to find high level jockeys and horses, in order to extend this type of year-round tourism. To this effect, the supply of this product has been diversified and prolonged, though to a lesser degree, than that of the previously mentioned spas. The nautical supply of the marinas, in the municipalities of Benalmádena, Marbella, Estepona, Malíva and, Fuengirola, in the western Costa del Sol, cannot be ignored either. Also, a large tourism industry of congresses, conventions and fairs has developed in the Costa del Sol. These latter types of tourism are not based on the supply of sea, sun, and sand, but are the foundation and reflection of the excellent supply of lodging and leisure in the region throughout the year.

Beginning with the Palace of Congresses of Torremolinos, there are also almost a score of hotel establishments, which have made a name for themselves, by providing at least 95 conference halls.

The municipality of Benalmádena has the largest consolidated number of tourists with sporting interests, such as tennis, hockey, baseball, cricket and soccer, sponsored by the Municipal Sports Association of Benalmádena. Following this example, all the municipalities, with some demographic significance, show development in this direction. The purpose of these sports' centers, in theory, is for the local residents, but in the last few years, they have fulfilled a double function of attracting the market of outside tourism.

Other recreational installations, complementary to the traditional supply of sea, sun and sand, would be the Tivoli World Amusement Park in Benalmádena. Those who look to explore a more ecological tourism can find the marine life park, of Sea Life, once again, in Benalmádena and the nature park Selwo, in Estepona, with thousands of animals living partially in the wild. The previously mentioned casinos are another attraction, which diversify the market. Other places of interest will be mentioned later in this book.

However, it is necessary to emphasize that the intention of making a commitment to bidding for complementary supplies and, thus, prolonging the summer vacation period in the region, is causing a great impact in the area. For one thing, the marinas are eliminating the extension of some beaches.

Some golf courses have destroyed areas of extremely high ecological value, as well as consuming enormous quantities of the scarce and exhaustible resource, which water represents. Also, the traffic congestion causes nuclei of contamination and noise.[9] These negative situations are completely contrary to what is desirable and are increased more in the high season. It is to be hoped that restrictions in the Costa de Sol will not have to be as radical as those placed on tourism in Spain, and in France, due to the damage done to the prehistoric cave paintings. Also, it can be hoped that nothing comparable will occur, in the Spanish coast, to the limits of growth imposed on the visits to Stonehenge, England, where the excess of tourism demand on the site caused its erosion.

---

[9] Op. Cit. 343

CHAPTER 2

The Forerunners of the Tourism Area Life Cycle Theory

This chapter contains a review of the academic literature, from whence the Tourism Area Life Cycle Theory has arisen and evolved. To this end, a review will be made, based on Butler's own recounting, of the most formative influences on his conceptual model. In the following chapter, examples of their empirical application will be identified.

THE HISTORICAL BEGINNINGS OF THE STUDY OF TOURISM

Butler affirms that in terms of the historicism relating to tourism studies, it is not unusual for the followers of the tourism phenomenon, to have reached the conclusion that the study of tourism is a recent field and relatively little research has been accomplished regarding it, before the decade of the 90's. Butler affirms that this is a distortion of reality, which undoubtedly, is a large component of why tourism studies suffer from a lack luster, academic reputation. Even, and mistakenly, the recognized researchers, in other scientific areas, peer into the arena of tourism, with the intention of publishing, basing themselves on the wrong presumption that there is new ground to be covered and enriched by their, sometimes, limited contributions.

Dramatic changes in the world of tourism took place in the decade of the 60's of the past century. These transformations were felt, to a large degree, in Great Britain, where British visitors began to abandon the spaces of leisure on their islands and ventured to the Mediterranean region for their fun and amusement. In the case of Spain, Mallorca was the pioneer, in attracting a considerable segment of the British tourism market, as well as that of Continental Europe.

From that time on, few people were aware of the magnitude that these changes would imply. Also, very little had been written about this dynamic. Within the little, yet budding literature, which existed on this subject. Butler highlights Gilbert (1939, 1954), Oglilvie (1933), Pimlott (1947), House (1954) and Barratt (1958), as all of them had touched upon and analyzed aspects of the development of tourism destination, their markets, their morphology, and their dynamics. [10]

These contributions, now unnoticed and underappreciated, were responsible for the fundamentals of the later work, which has been accomplished regarding tourism destinations. Butler rescues the morphology of Baratt's model of a tourism destination and considers it to be a creation prior to the theory of Stansfield and Rickert regarding

---

[10] Richard W. Butler, "The Concept of a Tourist Area Cycle of Evolution: Implications for Management of Resources," Review made by Butler, *The Tourism Area Life Cycle, Vol. 1, Applications and Modifications* (Cleveland: Channel View Publications, 2004), 4

districts of recreational business,[11] but it is when cited in the context of Mathieson and Wall (1982), in their theory on carrying capacity and cycles of tourism, where it is debated whether they are incipient theories or simply unfounded contradictions. For Butler, Barratt's structure is as valid, at the present time, as it was half a century ago. Thus, Butler reveals that the TALC arose from the background of the complexities of his personal experience, as well as from this small theoretical body.

THE ORIGIN OF THE TALC

The first moment, in which Butler's use of the terminology, "the cycle of a tourism destination" appears in print as already mentioned, is in a jointly presented paper by the latter and Jim Brougham, entitled, "The Applicability of the Asymptomatic Curve to the Forecasting of the Development of Tourism." It was presented in an annual meeting in Quebec City, in 1972, of the Travel Research Association. This work deserves a degree of mention, as in it, the basic points of the "Tourism Area Life Cycle Theory" are introduced. Therefore:

> ...from the point of view of predictions of flows of tourists, and the consequent growth of tourist destination areas, the need is greatest to explain the choice of specific locations, and the process of movement from one of the choice of specific locations, and the process of movement from one location to another over time.[12]

This paper, mainly, argues that more attention should be paid to the flow of tourists. This premise was based on Williams' and Zelinsky's theory (1970), and Yokeno's French study (1968) which has to do with the location of the tourism industry, and the application of the analysis to this phenomenon made by Thunen-Weber (1868). In this study, the following conclusion was arrived at, with reference to the study of Nice.

> A point will be reached, however, at which the rate of increase of visitors begins to decline and may even, as in the case above, become a decline in numbers. Such a trend may be due to a number of factors, such as increasing pollution, increasing land values limiting expansion of facilities, congestion of facilities, and the availability of alternative areas.[13]

As Butler himself affirms, it must be underlined that the main focus of this paper, which goes back to 1972, was the prediction of where tourism development would be found and where the spatial flows of population would be located. This, for Butler, was more of the focal point, than was the cycle of the destination, *per se*. No doubt, as a reflection of their geographic formation, Brougham and Butler, based themselves, upon Garrison's "rule of change," as Bunge says:

---

[11] Charles A. Stansfield et al., "The Recreational Business District," *Journal of Leisire Research,* Ibid, 20
[12] Jim Brougham et al., "The Applicability of the Asymptomatic Curve to the Forecasting of the Development of Tourism," (Presentation at the Travel Research Association, Quebec City, 1972)
[13] *Ibid.*, 6

Where capacity increase requires physical expansion, where the expansion cannot be in the vertical dimension and where the space is made more expensive by the presence of the phenomena itself, a shift is likely during times of capacity strain and the shift will probably occur to a new location as near to the old location as the area of induced expense will allow.[14]

It can be observed that this rule can be applied to the case of the Mediterranean, where the extensive expansion begins in the French Riviera, continuing through the Italian Riviera, then on to Spain (here it is worth noting the expansion, in particular, first throughout the Costa Brava and then to the Costa del Sol), after to the Adriatic Coast, and finally to North Africa. Afterwards, Malta, Cyprus and Turkey are, historically, incorporated into this phenomenon.

For Butler, Christaller's early contribution is also significant. Christaller affirms:

The typical course of development has the following pattern. Painters search out untouched and unusual places to paint. Step by step, the place develops as a so-called artist colony. Soon a cluster of poets follow, kindred to the painters: then cinema people, gourmets, and the jeunesse dorée. The place becomes fashionable and the entrepreneur takes note. The fisherman's cottage, shelter-huts become converted into boarding houses and hotels come on the scene.[15]

This author continues:

Meanwhile, the painters have fled and sought out another periphery--- periphery as related to space, and metaphorically, as 'forgotten' places and landscapes. Only the painters with a commercial inclination who like to do well in business remain; they capitalize on the good name of this former painter's corner and on the gullibility of tourists.[16]

According to Christaller, the space becomes a place where:

More and more townsmen choose this place, now en vogue and advertised in the newspapers. Subsequently the gourmets, and all those who seek real recreation, stay away. At last the tourist agencies come with their package rate travelling parties, now, the indulged public avoids such places. At the same time, in other place the same cycle occurs again: more and more places come into fashion, change their type, and turn into everybody's tourist haunt.[17]

---

[14] William Bunge, *Theoretical Geography* (London, C.W.K. Gleerup Publishers, 1966), 17
[15] Walter Christaller, *Beitrage zu einer Geographie der Fremdenverkehr* (Erdkunde, Band IX, Heft 1, 1955)
[16] Ibid., 2
[17] Ibid., 2.

Butler also states that the TALC is partly a product of Plog's frequently cited work (1973), which deals with the psycho-graphics of tourists. Having said this, Butler was not firm in conviction that its title ("Why Destination Areas Rise and Fall in Popularity") really did justice to the empirical study on which it was based. It dealt with a survey of North American travelers on what, or to the contrary, motivated them to fly.

This paper was first presented in the Travel Research Association of Southern California, in Los Angles. That is, in the same association where Brogham and Butler had given their presentation. The relevance of Plog's paper is that it created a model, where stipulations were made, on how changes in the tourism market, were related to consequential changes, in the destinations visited. It also included his statement, which is very frequently cited, that all tourism destinations are already incorporated with, from their insemination, their own destruction. The latter is, perhaps, the greatest contribution of this paper. Butler's presentation joined the group of the few affirmations, which touched upon the theme of destination decadence.

There are three other works, which were influential, in the establishment, of the TALC theory, which Butler cites in this compilation. The first, in order of importance, though last in chronological order of its publication, as it was published in 1978, was Stanfield's previously mentioned article. In this work, Stanfield analyzes and discusses the rise, fall, and later the resurgence of the destination due to institutionalized gambling, which was made legal there. Upon accomplishing this, he provided proof in academic literature of the cycle concept, as well as exemplifying a tourism destination, which reaches a process of rejuvenation. (Stanfield and Rickert, 1978).

Another article that Butler notes as, considerably, important for the development of the TALC was also Doxey's (1975), previously mentioned article, which was unveiled at the Travel Research Association's 6th Annual Conference, in San Diego, California. It expounded on his widely cited theory of the "Irridex."

Doxey's theory refers to an index of irritability. This index proposes a process of change with regard to the attitudes experienced by the local residents towards the tourists who are visiting in their locations. It suggests and follows the well-known behavioral adage that "familiarity breeds contempt." It is to say that, over time, the residents of a tourist destination will transform their reaction to the presence of these outsiders, in their space, from one of a positive reaction to that of a negative nature.

In 1975, Butler was, already, discussing the validity of this theory affirming that it was too simplistic. It is, however, undeniable that the suggestion, in the article, that tourism spaces, as well as the attitudes of the residents, regarding these tourists, change, throughout the development of the industry, complement, as well as enhance the very scarce literature dealing with this subject matter that was available at the time.

The negative shift of the Costa del Sol's native residents' public opinion, which is even manifested, extensively, nation-wide is a reflection, as well as a reaction to the enormous consumption of water, which is used to maintain the golf courses expansive emerald green color. At the same time, though it is not quantifiable, a certain antagonism exists between the nationals and the tourists from abroad, during the high summer seasons, when the visiting population is greater than that of the residents.

The third article mentioned by Butler and which clarifies, to a great degree, the process of change in tourism destinations, was a publication, written by Roy Wolfe, which stands out over those of his peers. Wolfe was known as an authority in subjects versing on recreation and tourism, in the 60's and 70's, in the Canadian and North American realm.

According to Butler, this researcher has not been given the full credit he is due. Wolfe focused his studies on vacation homes, in Ontario, (1948). His work was, in reality, and according to Butler, the link between "current" and "antiquated" tourism studies. Roy Wolfe, also contributed to a very superior study, by comparison, to those of his time. This was a joint project he embarked upon with the government of Ontario highway models.

However, what most definitely influenced Butler, according to himself, in the concept of the cycle, was Wolfe's publication on Wasaga Beach (1952), a classical café tourism destination, which he discussed in his "Separation from the Geographical Setting," in which he traced its development from a peaceful town populated with second homes, to a recreational, and tourism destination, which is what Ontario is in the present.

Here, he confirms the importance of the town, and the manner and form, in which development changes the role and importance of the natural aspects of the appeal of a destination, and the influence of exogenous factors in tourism patterns. This article (Wolfe 1952) was a pioneer in this subject, when published in The Canadian Geographer, almost three decades before the original TALC.

This transformation can be applied, not only to the Costa del Sol, but to other tourism destinations, along the Spanish Mediterranean coastline. Specifically, Torremolinos stands out as a typification, of this form of spatial development, upon its transition from a sleepy village in the '50's and early '60's, to becoming what it is today---a noisy, massively, crowded and enormously popular tourism destination. It is the representation par excellence, in the Costa del Sol, of a form of tourism that is both friendly, yet tinny, at the same time. This particular case will be analyzed, ahead, in another section of this book.

Butler unveils his environmentalist side, upon revealing that the literature of ecology and of the populations of flora and fauna also must be added to the list of theoretical bodies, limited at that time, referring to the development of tourism destinations, which were influential in the conception of the TALC. There are existing analogies between these, and the cycles of populations.

For Butler, there are similarities which lie, on one hand, between the tourism destination, which grows rapidly and without apparent consideration for the preservation of its resources and population, and on the other, the flora and fauna, which increase without naturally respecting the future and the capacity of the environment to sustain its own vital advancement.

In this sense, Butler is a pioneer in the combination of ecology and sociology, which is both a tribute and a result of his own experience as an observer of nature.

This acquired and experiential insight, no doubt, influenced his elaboration of the conceptual framework of the evolution of the life of a tourism destination.

Even though, considering the previous discussion, it may seem that Brougham and Butler, in 1972, coined the term of "the cycle of a tourism destination." Yet, even before the previously mentioned Stansfield (1978), the concept of a process, consistent with the development and change of tourism destination, with recognizable phases and stages, dates back to over a century ago. Without any self-aggrandizement, and to this point, Butler declares that, in the London Times, an article appeared in an 1860 issue that discussed the process of development of a tourism destination. So, it reads:

> Our seaport towns have been turned inside out. So infallible and unchanging are the attractions of the ocean that it is enough for any place to stand on the shore. That one recommendation is sufficient. Down comes the Excursion Train with its thousands--- some with a month's range, others tethered to a six hours' limit, but all rushing with one impulse to the waters' edge.

And so, this article continues:

> Where are they to lodge? The old 'town' is perhaps half a mile inland and turned as far away from the sea as possible...But this does not suit visitors whose eyes are always on the waves, and so a new town arises on the beach. Marine Terraces, Sea Villas, 'Prospect Lodges', 'Bellevues', hotels baths, libraries and churches soon accumulate, till at length of the old borough is completely hidden and perhaps to be reached by an omnibus.[18]

As a postscript, Butler also finds a 19th century observation, regarding this subject, in an editorial in the magazine, *The Nation*, one of the most renowned progressive publications, since its establishment in 1865 until the present, in the United States. The piece was entitled, "Evolution of the Summer Boarder," and states, as follows:

> The growth of the American watering place, indeed, now seems to be as much regulated by law as the growth of asparagus or strawberries and is almost as easy to foretell. The place is usually first discovered by artists... or a family of small needs in search of pure air...[19]

The editor continues to describe a process of development, which begins with the supply of unstructured lodging, followed by public advertising, the transformation of country farms to hotels (this stage takes about 30 to 40 years, according to Godkin), and concludes with the arrival of the masses and crowds.

Later comes the construction of vacation homes, which are built on the same land sold by the farmer. In this process, the renter has no other alternative, but to search

---

[18] Richard Butler, *the London Times*, 1860, 10/9, 2006, 6.
[19] E.L. Godkin, "Evolution of the Summer Boarder," *The Nation*, comment on Butler R. Op. Cit., 47-48

out other farmsteads that have not gone through this sophisticated process of transformation.

Godkin speaks to the great tragedy of the disappearing summer American life-style, when referring to the less affluent tenants' who lose their opportunities of rest and relaxation, now, because the existing presence of the wealthy owners' vacation homes. This editorial caused quite a stir of correspondence, both in favor and against, this postulate. However, this literature, with its consequential correspondence, demonstrates that the polemic regarding this subject matter had already been established at such a remote time. The discussion even continued in *The Nation* for a considerable number of subsequent years.

Butler also returns to Conrad Hobbs' work of 1915, when he revisits the theory of the evolution of a tourism destination in the Worcester Magazine. Here, it is worth noting an explanation of the process because of its descriptive clarity. It is explained, *a grosso modo*, with the following characteristics:

1. The destination is enjoyed by a few.
2. The destination's population increases, and symptoms of abuse begin to appear.
3. The abuse increases and there is degradation of the place, which leads to,
4. A greater appreciation for its latent, though diminished value, and the public's demand for its conservation, which if it has sufficient strength and persistence, may end in,
5. Its recovery, and protection under a strong and efficient control[20]

At the same time, Butler clarifies why an article such as one that deals with tourism, and specifically with the TALC, would have appeared in *The Canadian Geographer*, a publication which usually does not publish material of this type.

This peculiarity is due to the fact that the original presentation of the TALC was made at an annual conference of the Association of Canadian Geographers in Vancouver in 1980. At that time, it was the case that for the first time in the history of its publication, a special edition was published, devoted to tourism and leisure. One of the articles included in this unprecedented published text so fortunately contained the theory, upon which this study verses itself.

THE RELEVANCE OF THE TALC IN THE PRESENT

Before closing this section, it is worth raising the question as to why the TALC has maintained its utility and popularity for over the last two decades. Aside from what has been determined to be its "elegant" form, perhaps its usefulness is its most outstanding quality. In the first place, it is a very easy model to apply, and at the same time, it is able to welcome, with much flexibility, many forms of information. In this

---

[20] See Butler R. *Ibid.* 35

book, the TALC has been used to perform spatial, as well as temporal, dimensions of analysis.

Also, it is intuitively, as well as appropriately, useful as a comfortable "hanger," from which to attach numerous studies of diverse, yet specific, destinations. This facet of the TALC makes it an outstanding tool, upon completing a study, such as the one, established in this book, when applying it to the Spanish Costa del Sol. This theory's validity also extends itself to other fields, which examine even more specific spaces.

In second place, the TALC appeared on the scientific stage, when viable models and concepts applicable to the field of tourism were lacking and were avidly sought out. As such, the study of this science evolved from a more merely descriptive phase to another of increasing description, and conceptual analysis.

That being said, and as was mentioned previously, it is a model, which is flexible and very capable of adapting, as well as, at the same time, modifying itself, to maintain its relevance, within the context of the concepts of sustainable tourism and those of appropriate development. It has been and continues to prove itself to be valid and acceptable under many scientific premises.

Thirdly, in the final analysis, the TALC is a study of the evolvement of human nature, and their behavioral activity, in the environment, when indiscriminately pursuing their needs of recreation and leisure in an advanced and industrialized society. The pursuit of these past times, like so many other socio-economic quests of the "civilized" world, can prove damaging to the environment if not examined and controlled.

Therefore, the TALC, serves as a barometer, which defines and evaluates the level of sustainability of an activity, enacted in a tourist destination. This dimension of information can be acquired, both in spatial realm, as well as the temporal. The aim of this book is the study of the sustainability of the practice of golf on the Spanish Costa del Sol.

CHAPTER 3

Theoretical and Empirical Application of the Theory

INTRODUCTION

Analyzing the studies which refer to this theory is not an easy undertaking, nor is it an exact science, as upon embarking upon this venture, multiple criteria may be manipulated. A form of organization could be to disclose, in chronological order, when their content was exposed to the scientific world. Also, the studies could be divided in opposite categories, that is to say, those which support the Tourism Area Life Cycle Theory, and those that do not. Also, an exposé could be done, according to levels and what methodologies have been used in their application, or to which stages of the cycle they have directed their implementation of the theory. At the same time, the possibility of making a visual analysis of the studies, thereby simplifying their access through the means of visual graphics, charts, etc. could be formed.

THE ANALYSIS OF EMPIRICAL AND THEORETICAL CASES

Gary Hovinen's study (1981) of Lancaster County, in the state of Pennsylvania, was the first in applying the TALC, and the first to be analyzed, by Lawgiewski in his article. This county has a long history, as has already been expounded, in another chapter of this investigative study.

Hovinen arrived at the conclusion that this tourism destination significantly diverted from the TALC in its final stages. However, he agrees that it maintains its utility to a certain point. Thus:

> Perhaps Butler's model is most successfully applied to certain conventional resort destinations that undergo cycles of evolution. A cycle is certainly discernible in Lancaster County, but the highly diversified nature of tourism that currently exists and the fact that there are different elements of the tourist industry which are at different stages of the cycle makes it difficult to distinguish between consolidation, stagnation, and decline.[21]

Hovinen continues, with the following:

> Earlier stages of exploration, involvement, and development with many of the characteristics suggested by Butler in his 1989 formulation are clearly

---

[21] Gary Hovinen, "Lancaster County, the TALC, and the Search for Sustainable Tourism," 75. Butler RW, *Ibid.*, 73-90

discernable. But the county tourism industry is now mature and highly diversified, and problems arise when trying to fit the tourism trends of the past quarter century to Butler's assumptions of a progression to later stages of consolidation, stagnation, and then either possible decline or complete rejuvenation.[22]

The definition of the maturity phase is the most noteworthy stage of the theory. It is even applicable to the Spanish Costa del Sol, which may be considered a mature destination, upon having diversified its resources with the transformation of the supply of the product. Beginning with the basic and simple supply of sea, sun and sand, this coastline has continued to develop, the already mentioned, marinas, golf courses, spas, sports arenas and other attractions.

As Hovinen, in his study on Lancaster County, substitutes the decline phase for the more complex stage of maturity, he reasons that its proximity to important cities along the East Coast, allows it to attract even more visitors. Also, its tourist base is diverse, due to the fact that the visitors are not only and entirely attracted by the Amish community, but to the same degree, by other cultural and geographical factors, such as the rural landscape in and of itself.

The proximity of the Costa del Sol to other European countries, such as Germany and Great Britain, make this a destination with a very diverse demand. It is more competitive, in the international market than, for example, Cyprus or Turkey, as well as other North African countries. Also, the diversified supply of tourism attractions, such as golf courses, to mention only one, represent a very wide array of these available in the Costa del Sol, in addition to the traditional three S's—Sea, Sun and Sand. This reflects the validity of Hovinen's maturity theory, which allows the TALC to be refined and applied to this Spanish coast.

Hovinen continues to modify Butler's Life Cycle Theory, proposing that the "chaos/complexity theory" allows for a useful and complementary alternative to the TALC. This theory is based on Russell and Faulkner's (1999) conception, which implies that changes in a tourism destination may be interpreted in terms of the tension created between entrepreneurs (the agents of change) and planners, and regulators (those whose intent is to control change).

The Australian scientists express the following:

> The chaos perspective has provided a useful framework for analyzing the history of tourism development on the Gold Coast, one of Australia's major seaside resorts. Here, specific phases in tourism development can be associated with the actions of individual entrepreneurs, who were responsible for an innovation that initiated a sequence of changes culminating in a major shift in the structure of tourism activities.[23]

They continue:

---

[22] *Ibid.*, 89
[23] Roslyn Russell et al., "Movers and Shakers: Chaos Makers in Tourism Development," *Tourism Management*, no. 20 (August 1999): 411-423

The sequence of changes that the Gold Coast has experienced can, therefore, be interpreted in terms of the tension between the entrepreneurs (the chaos makers) and planners and regulators (the dampeners), whose actions are generally focused on moderating and controlling change. Periods of rapid change, which are characterized by the chaos perspective occur when the chaos makers prevail over the dampeners.[24]

They suggest their business instincts are crucial because, in order to avoid a state of decline of a tourist area, innovative responses are needed to confront the complexities, which a tourism destination faces, as it nears the decline stage or, for Hovinen, the maturity phase. At the same time, the role of planners and regulators is necessary so that the process of tourism development will not go uncontrolled and will be maintained in a situation of sustainable growth. This early study on Lancaster County is, perhaps, the most noted among experts because it proposed a maturity phase as an alternative to the decline phase and it incorporates it into the TALC.

Haywood's study (1986), which also appears in Lagiewski's article, has often been cited as a work, which reflects a critical position taken regarding Butler's model of the TALC. In spite of this scientist's negative scrutiny and probing into Butler's premise it has caused quite the opposite effect. This additional analysis of the TALC formulated a sort of removal of the theoretical creases and performed a dry cleaning of the conceptual model creating a sleek and smoothly finished fabric of the position.

In this regard, Haywood believes that the TALC's true litmus test is: "However, the true test of the importance of the life cycle must be based on its possible use as a tool for the planning and management of tourist areas."[25]

He continues to expound in his article that, in order to make the TALC an operative model, six points of analysis must be included in it. They are the following:

In order to make the tourist-area life cycle operational, six major conceptual and measurement decisions need to be considered:

- Unit of Analysis;
- Relevant Market;
- Pattern and Stages of the Tourist Area of Life Cycle;
- Identification of the Area's Shape in the Cycle;
- Determination of the Unit of Measurement;
- Determination of the Relevant Time Unit.[26]

Regarding the first point, Haywood finds that it is surprising how such very little attention was given to define the unit of analysis, which the TALC applies to the tourism destination. The first point has to do with the definition and delineation of the tourism area in question. That is to say, this author states that the first step consists in

---

[24] Ibid., 411
[25] M.K. Haywood, "Can the Tourist Life Cycle Be Made Operational?," *Tourism Management*, no. 3 (1988): 154
[26] *Ibid.,* Haywood, 156

defining the unit of analysis of the "tourism area," when using Butler's life cycle model. With reference to the second point, which has to do with the quality of the tourists, Haywood writes the following:

> Most applications of the tourist-area life cycle assume implicitly that the tourist market is homogeneous and composed primarily of one segment with district sub segments that differ from each other only in their degree of 'innovativeness'.[27]

He continues:

> While most tourist area life studies have focused on visitation at the total market level, there are occasions in which it may be appropriate and important to consider the resort area life-cycle by market type (e.g. domestic versus international tourists), distribution method (e.g. travel agent versus independent booking) or market segment (e.g. family versus corporate group).[28]

Haywood's third premise has to do with the "S" formed curve, on which Butler's TALC bases itself. Butler's analogy is a novel one when it is applied to the life of a tourism destination, but it has already been applied to other scientific realms, such as that of biological evolution. Haywood questions its validity when applying it to the tourism arena, in the following terms:

> The existence of a variety of non-S-shaped curve patterns implies that there are other than the traditional stages to this tourist-area life cycle. In fact, even those who accept the S-shaped curve as the dominant pattern of tourist-area-life-cycle of evolution identify a varying number of stages of labels for these stages.[29]

The following conceptualization from Haywood deals with the consideration of the manner, in which one stage transitions into another. The researcher poses the following doubt:

> Given that time series data rarely obey the theoretical patterns of a smooth curve, and that the S-shaped curve is only one of a number of a number of possible life-cycle patters, it is not at all clear whether a tourist area's position in its cycle and its shift from stage to another can be identified simply by observing the historical pattern of the number of tourist.[30]

Haywood resolves this by basing himself on aspects of the TALC:

---

[27] *Ibid.,* Haywood, 156
[28] *Ibid.,* Haywood, 156
[29] *Ibid.,* Haywood, 157
[30] *Ibid.,* Haywood, 158

Identifying the length of time of each stage and the exact point at which a tourist area shifts from one stage to another is closely related to the use of the tourist-area-life-cycle concept for forecasting visitation rates, market accessibility and acceptance and actions of competitive tourist areas.[31]

The fifth measure of analysis is the definition of an appropriate unit with which estimation may be made of when the saturation of the carrying capacity has been reached. Therefore, Haywood proposes that if the number of tourists who visit the destination will be used as the barometer, then also the following points should be considered:

- the length of stay;
- the dispersion of tourists within and throughout the tourist area;
- the characteristics of the tourists; and finally,
- the time of year, in which the visit is made.[32]

He also believes that the operating businesses' level of profit in the tourist region might represent an interesting measure. This may lend itself to establish, at what point of the cycle, the destination finds itself, even though, without any doubt, this figure would be difficult to obtain in the space to be studied.

Haywood considers another possibility, in the following terms:

The second issue concerns the appropriateness of using a tourist-expenditure model instead of tourist population to determine the shape pattern and stage of the life cycle. If such a measure were used a subsequent question would be whether this expenditure should measure unit sales (e.g. number of visits to a park or museum) or dollar value. Then of course, this is the question as to whether the analysis of this expenditure should be based on actual expenditure or adjusted expenditure.[33]

He continues to ponder:

For example, should they be adjusted per capita expenditure? Corrected for seasonal or cyclical periods. Adjusted for general economic conditions (e.g. current versus real prices?[34]

The norm should be to have an analysis made of the tourism area using the annual criteria. However, Haywood differs in this regard. In his sixth point, he bases himself on Butler's premise that the increase in the number of tourists negatively affects the carrying capacity, but on the other hand, he suggests the need for a clear and

---

[31] *Ibid.*, Haywood, 158
[32] *Ibid.*, 159
[33] Ibid., 159
[34] *Ibid.*, 159

transparent unit of measure—which defines, as well as qualifies—the quantity and, at the same time, specifies the quality of these same tourists.

Haywood bases himself on the abundantly known fact that not all tourists have the same impact on the carrying capacity of the tourist destination, which they visit. That is to say, not all tourists are created equally. Some stay for a longer visit, while others arrive in different seasons. Some even have more of an awareness and respect, and of course, others less for the cultural and natural traditions of the place. Here a point can be made regarding the bad reputation that the Costa del Sol acquired in the 70's, due to its tourists' poor public behavior.

To this end, the number of sheer arrivals is questioned, as the determining factor of the carrying capacity of a tourism destination. Haywood believes that a dangerous numerical simplification may be arrived at, if the tourists are not analyzed qualitatively. He also reflects upon whether there exists just one variable, which represents the carrying capacity for the whole tourism area.

In the Costa del Sol, it can be said that there is one factor or variable, which determines the entire tourism area's carrying capacity. That is the consumption of water of its coast, lined with nearly a hundred golf courses back-to-back. At the rate of their water consumption, these courses individually determine the destination's carry capacity, which in this case is environmental. In all, Haywood's elaboration upon the study of the tourism destination, neglects to define or even mention the environmental carrying capacity, as a factor to be reckoned with, as a basic criterion, for the analysis of the development of any tourism destination.

In his article, Lagiewski also touches upon Strapp's study of Sauble Beach, located in the province of Ontario, Canada, (1988). This study is acknowledged because of its contribution to the TALC, through the recognition of the role "vacation home owners" play in the cycle. Among other concepts, which this scientist touches upon and alludes to is the importance of these players, in opposition to the conventional type of short-term tourism. The increase of this type of housing could alter the stage of decline by converting it into the rejuvenation stage of a tourism destination.

Strapp writes:

> In summary, the great decline and stagnation in the number of conventional tourists experienced in Sauble Beach has not been reflected in an overall diminution of the community's health because of two factors. First, a substantial increase in the amount of time spent in the community after the traditional tourist season has enabled the community to broaden its economic base, beyond the unstable summer market.[35]

He continues conveying the second factor:

---

[35] James D. Strapp, "The Resort Cycle and Second Homes," *Annals of Tourism Research*, no. 4 (1988): 511-512.

Second, the increase net economic benefit derived from a different form of visitor has counteracted the absolute decline in numbers. As a result, Sauble Beach is rightly thought by its residents to be a growing community.[36]

This is also perceived, in the Costa del Sol, where a lack of growth of "conventional" tourists has been witnessed and there is an increase in the birth of housing developments. In many cases, these developments are situated on the edges of the golf courses. A "new-range of supply" of these types of properties has been made available since the 80's. Among these, it is difficult to distinguish which are the secondary residences and which are the rentals.

In this case, what can be said with difficulty, is that many of the residents are foreign property owners who are originally from Great Britain, Germany, the Netherlands, as well as the Nordic countries. These properties allow for larger profits on the regional economic scene, while simultaneously requiring many more natural resources, such as water. It can be said that there is a dysfunctional relationship between financial expenditure for real estate and the expenditure these properties make of the natural, as well as scarce resource, in this, the region of "Dry Spain."

Alejandro López López had already noted this fact in one of his articles when he said:

> The spatial models of residency occupy more space, generate more demands on mobility, multiply the needs of infrastructure, and the allocations of structures. At the same time, they decrease the efficiency of the environmental and energy investments. In this territorial framework, the present tourist activity is based primarily on the promotion of real estate holding, supported by the holiday model of beach and sun.[37]

And López López continues:

> This implies maintaining an empty housing development, during three fourths of the year, with all the urban facilities, only functioning 25% of this time, with much consumption of space, elevated degradation of the environment, and with very little yield and cost effectiveness for the local population.[38]

With the intent of refining Butler's model, Strapp suggests optional inroads to the stagnation stage or the rejuvenation stage.

> At the critical stagnation stage, three general options are possible, not necessarily related directly to a decline or rejuvenation of tourism. The simplest to conceptualize is a continued shortening of time spent as the area

---

[36] Ibid., Strapp, 512

[37] Alejandro López López, "Otra mirada, turismo y medioambiente," *La contra, tribuna Complutense*, May 24, 2005, 24

[38] *Ibid.*, López López, 26

declines and becomes more of a recreational area or rest stop. Many older European and Eastern North American resorts, such as Blackpool (United Kingdom) appear to have experienced this stage.[39]

And Strapp continues:

Another option is associated with a rejuvenation of tourist attractions. The visit time regains its length as other resources are exploited, as in Atlantic City. The actual time spent is a function of the type of attraction offered, but its position between the other options in terms of length of stay is consistent.[40]

Thus, according to Strapp:

The final option, a move to more year-round residency, is the one followed in Sauble Beach. This most applicable to cottage resorts where the infrastructure for such a transition already exists. The area becomes more of a residential community with people staying well past the traditional tourist season. Consequently, the length of time spent in the community increases dramatically.[41]

Therefore, Strapp proposes that the transition from a situation of "holiday homes" to "year-round homes" allows for a more stable phase in the destination.
    He writes:

The conversion of cottages and addition of year-round homes should, therefore, more appropriately be termed a stabilization process. The process is characterized by a leveling off of tourism levels and an increase in off season residential use of the area.[42]

It may be deduced, as Strapp suggests, that the possibility of entering the phase of decline may increase, upon the tourists having easier access to the destination, by airports, trains, and seaports. In this manner, the trips are shortened, and in his theory, the greater opportunity to make one-day trips increases as the stagnation phase approaches. It can be assumed that, when spending just one day in the place, the tourist does not become identified with the visited space, and even views it as a merely disposable object.
    Consequently, as is mentioned in another section of this book, the effects of the bullet train, AVE, has on the Costa del Sol, has yet to be determined. This train provides a quick means for a short stay to this, now desirable, destination. It is possible that this means of transportation that facilitates these "mini-vacations," in

---

[39] *Op. Cit.*, Strapp, 512
[40] *Ibid.*, Strapp, 512
[41] *Ibid.*, Strapp pp. 512
[42] *Ibid,.* Strapp pp. 512

this resort destination, may be responsible for increasing its quantity of visitors, but, also their quality, which may lead, at some point, to the threshold of its decline.

Parallelisms may be drawn between the Costa del Sol, and the Sauble Beach study, as defined, in its third option, that is to say, when the tourist becomes a resident. In the Costa del Sol the tourist season stretches throughout the entire year. It is, also, one of the largest regions in Europe to welcome retired immigrants from such areas as, Great Britain, Germany, the Benelux Union, and the Nordic nations.

As in similar regions, there is a dialectical relationship between the receiving community and the foreign arrivals. Rodriguez et al. (1998) studied the principal British and Nordic citizen's reasons behind their permanent migration to Spain. The results showed that these were, already, homeowners, when they made their decision to take up permanent residency there, after their retirement. It was, also, discovered, through this study, that this population found it to be more affordable to rent a house in the Costa del Sol during the winter than pay for high heating expenses, in their country of origin.

Thus, this indicates the following:

> The winter warmth of the Costa del Sol also means that heating costs are much less than in Europe, an important consideration for those whose income is decreasing. As one respondent stated, 'If we had stayed in England we wouldn't be living in the house where we lived because it was too big for two people and very expensive to heat.[43]

In general, the retired residents have benefited from the climate, the more relaxed Spanish lifestyle, and the cheaper cost of living. The regional economy of the area has benefitted primarily from the British, as they purchase either plots of land, apartments or houses. In doing so, they have increased their expenditures in appliances, furnishings and services. They have also been the responsible parties for the creation of jobs in construction and maintenance.

This symbiotic relationship between the national economy and its foreign resident retirees culminated in the concession of voting rights in local elections to this growing and influential population. This astounding situation proves that the level of interaction between both groups exceeds that of a simple tourism phenomenon, concerning a particular tourism season.

Even though, the TALC is not applied, in this article, *per se*, it may be suggested that the consolidation and stagnation stages are replaced by an extensive period of maturity, as by Foster and Murphy (1991), included in Lagiewski's article. Foster and Murphy discuss Strapp's previously mentioned article, which analyzes the conversion phenomenon of conventional tourism in Canada to permanent residents. These scientists call the Western flank of this country, "the banana band," because of its, comparatively, mild temperatures. They decidedly affirm that, here, the phenomenon of retirement is occurring parallel to that of tourism.

---

[43] Vicente Rodríguez *et. al.,* "European Retirees on the Costa del Sol: A Cross-National Comparison," *International Journal of Population Geography, no.* 4 (1998): 186

Their quote follows: "Retirees are attracted to many of the same features and locations as tourists, and communities have undertaken a variety of strategies to accommodate this market segment."[44]

The two authors performed a study of Parksville and Qualicum Beaches, where both locations are situated on the Eastern coast of the island of Vancouver. Their goal was to determine if these destinations follow Butler's premise. When a conventional tourist area becomes populated by communities of retirees, these scientists maintains that it will have already entered into the stagnation stage.

Foster and Murphy conclude, in contrast to Butler, that their research is supported by Hovinen (1982, 1995, 1997, 2002, 2006), in that the stages of stagnation and consolidation have been replaced by an extensive stage of maturity.

To this end, they write:

> This article has examined the appropriateness of Butler's (1980) model in explaining the development of two long-established resort communities on Vancouver Island, with particular reference to its relationship to retirement. It notes that the model provides a good description of early tourism trends, but that Hovinen's modification would be a more accurate description of later development patterns.[45]

Foster and Murphy continue, by writing: "Instead of appearing in the 'decline' stage, a growing retirement sector has been evident during tourism's 'development stage'."[46]

They conclude their article by underlining the importance that communities of retirees have on tourist destinations, especially now that the aging population is increasing globally.

Though this theory was applied to Canada, it is also applicable to the Costa del Sol. As previously mentioned, it is a well-known fact that in this area of Spain, there is a large population of retirees from Northern European countries. According to Foster and Murphy, it may be affirmed that the presence of this group does not imply, to any degree, that this destination has entered into the stagnation phase of the TALC. On the contrary, it signifies that the space is in the development stage.

Lagiewski (1997) includes Douglas and Butler's life cycle model in his study. He expounds upon the capacity of this model to explain the development of tourism in colonial and postcolonial societies. Douglas's main contribution to this research is that having to do with the natives already living in the place. It specifically refers to Butler's premise regarding the participation stage, where the contact between this group and the visitors will be high.

The presumption is that while Butler did not specifically define the concept of residents in his model, the implication was that it referred to the native population of the tourism area. Here, Douglas does not coincide with the idea that the residents need be native:

---

[44] Danny M. Foster et al., "Resort Cycle Revisited: The Retirement Connection," *Annals of Tourism Research*, no. 18 (1991): 554

[45] *Ibid.*, Foster et al., pp 565

[46] *Ibid.*, Foster et al., pp. 565.

Butler does not give a specific definition for 'locals'. But the implication is that he means 'indigenous' which is quite inappropriate for Melanesia. Apart from occasionally selling curios or giving a rare guided tour of a village house, the Melanesians had no contact with, or imput into tourism at all.[47]

Spain has never been a colony, but it is worth mentioning the application of this scientific model in order to develop a comparative study to Papua, New Guinea, the Solomon Islands and Vanuatu (Melanesia), and the Costa del Sol. To this point, Rodríguez et al. emphasizes the separation and alienation, also, experienced, by the foreign residents of the Costa del Sol, due to their lack of knowledge of the language. These authors write the following:

> Language was considered to be a key disadvantage of living on the Costa del Sol by 71%, and 51% gave it as a prime disadvantage. This opinion was most widespread amongst the British and least amongst the Belgian, German, and Dutch respondents.[48]

As an indication of the desire of the foreigners to participate in local life and activities, the following was determined in this study:

> In contrast to the general attachment to the Spanish life style, only a quarter of the respondents considered that *getting to know* the Spanish people was a positive aspect of living in the Costa del Sol, somewhat higher than the number who mentioned the advantage of meeting people from their own or other European nations.[49]

And they continue:

> Retired people from the Nordic and Benelux countries were more likely to value positively becoming acquainted with the Spanish, whereas the British and Germans were more likely to value the opportunities for meeting their fellow nationals.[50]

Though Butler did not specifically define the concept of residents in his model it is understood that he was referring to the local population of the tourism area. However, in terms of the historical development of tourism, the expatriates of the original colonies can be defined as the "locals." The European tourists prefer to interact and establish relationships with the European expatriates and not necessarily with the Melanesians.

---

[47] Ngaire Douglas, "Applying the Life Cycle Model to Melanesia," *Annals of Tourism Research*, no.1 (1997): 8-9.
[48] Vicente Rodríguez, *op cit.,* 191
[49] *Ibid,* 191
[50] *Ibid.,* 191

As has been discussed, the same phenomenon occurs in the Costa del Sol. The tourists prefer to interact with those "of their own kind." This would be an anomaly in the application of the TALC to the Costa del Sol. It could indicate a phase of "pre-stagnation," which is what this study intends to demonstrate, as well as create. This situation may also indicate that this region is not a "mature" destination, as some scientists have convened upon.

Another theory is based on Martin and Uysal's (1990) new conceptualization of the life cycle. These scientists base themselves on the premise that there are many components, which make up a tourism destination. Their major concern, however, has to do with the carrying capacity, a term, which is used by Alejandro López López, and defined by these authors in the following manner:

> ...carrying capacity can be defined as the number of visitors that an area can accommodate before negative impacts occur, whether to the physical environment, the psychological attitude of the tourist, or the social acceptance of the hosts. Physical carrying capacity involves two areas. These are the actual physical limitations of the area, the point at which not one more person can be accommodated. It also includes any physical deterioration of the environment which is caused by tourism.[51]

The article continues: "Psychological carrying capacity has been exceeded when tourists are no longer comfortable in the destination area, for reasons that can include perceived negative attitudes of the locals, crowding of the area, or deterioration in the physical environment."[52]

Then, for these scientists, the final form of carrying capacity is the social carrying capacity, which they define as: "Social capacity is reached when the local residents of an area no longer want tourists because they are destroying the environment, damaging the local culture or crowding them out of local activities."[53]

In order to determine these capacities, it is necessary, according to Martin and Uysal to analyze the destination by applying the TALC to it. Thus, they continue by, profoundly and tellingly, indicating:

> It is impossible to determine the tourism carrying capacity outside of the context of the position of the destination area in the life cycle. The interrelationship of the two concepts is dynamic. The carrying capacity for a destination area is different for each life cycle.[54]

---

[51] B.S. Martin et al., "An Examination of the Relationship between Carrying Capacity and the Tourism Life Cycle: Management and Policy Implications," *Journal of Environmental Management and Policy Implications*, no. 31 (1990): 329.
[52] *Ibid.*, 329.
[53] *Ibid.*, 329.
[54] *Ibid.*, 329.

Therefore, the position of the destination, within the life cycle is joined, and at the same time, related to different elements, which determine and affect it. In this way, it is difficult to define and measure the carrying capacity of each tourism space.

However:

> There is always at least one factor which sets the limit to the carrying capacity of an area, but not necessarily only one factor. It is possible to have facilities developed so as to accommodate many tourists, but for there to be environmental, social and economic problems. It is just as possible to have a great social rapport between host communities and the tourist, while facilities or infrastructure problems create negative feelings for the tourist.[55]

This theory can be applied to the Costa del Sol, given the fact that the limited, natural water resource is an ingredient that contains a carrying capacity which differs from the variable, of the physical infrastructure, such as those of hotel beds. With the present rate both of individual, as well as water consumption used for the irrigation of golf courses, it can be predicted that, in the foreseeable future, the availability of this scarce resource will be exhausted. On the other hand, the hotels' vertical construction, which contains the coastline's infrastructure, cannot exhaust its carrying capacity until a very distant future.

In Klaus J. Meyer-Arendt's study (1985), also cited by Richard Lagiewski, this ecologist explores the factors which pertain to matters which cause a destination to transition through all the stages of development, ending in the phase of stagnation. In his study, he emphasizes the patterns of settlement, the changes of environmental perceptions of the residents, as well as of the planners and administrators, on the Grand Isle in Louisiana, in order to create a dynamic coast.

Meyer-Arendt writes:

> The evolution of Grand Isle as a seaside resort can be described by the resort cycle model proposed by Butler (1980). Each stage of the cycle is characterized by distinctive settlement patterns that reflect changing environmental perceptions and/or conditions in addition to a real expansion...[56]

This author continues:

> From an initial settlement nestled among the higher beach ridges and focused toward the back bay and away from the environmentally hazardous beachfront tourism development extended out to the shore and into the

---

[55] *Ibid.*, pp. 330

[56] Klaus J. Meyer-Arendt, "The Grand Isle, Louisiana Resort Cycle," *Annals of Tourism Research*, no. 1 (1986): 462-463.

exposed vicinage zone. With construction of a beach highway settlement spread laterally and gradually intensified.[57]

As a result:

> Environmental degradation in the form of beach ridge leveling and driftwood removal accelerated the shoreline retreat process that originally created Grand Isle. Summer home construction along the dynamic beachfront led to a need to stabilize the seashore.[58]

Consequentially: "The efforts to accomplish this led to the tampering with beach processes that locally accelerated erosion even further, reduced the aesthetic appeal of the island and propelled Grand Isle into the advanced stages of the resort cycle."[59]

This article deserves consideration, in this context, as it completely accepts the application of TALC to a tourist destination. Given the fact, and according to Meyer-Arendt that the Grand Isle has already entered into the decadence phase, its future depends on an investment project of $14 million for the protection of the beach.

Parallelisms may be found between this area of the Southern state of Louisiana and the Costa del Sol. The latter has also fought a battle to conserve its beaches, as this is one of the most developed coastlines on the globe. During the last forty years, the majority of this natural space has been destroyed and substituted for urban services related to tourism. To this end, towering edifices of apartment buildings, hotels and condominiums have been built.

This urban coastline was a battleground, from the beginning, when engineers tried to undermine its progressive erosion by means of the construction of sea walls, breakwaters and different designs for partitioning the beach. These structures have functioned on a scale from being only satisfactory to totally unacceptable, as in certain areas they have exacerbated the beach loss and have added to the coastal recession. In Marbella and Estepona, the breakwaters, which were built in the 60's, were removed later, in favor of stabilizing the beach.

The depleting of physical resources can be attributed to the skyrocketing increase of the demand placed on water and its aggregates. The scarcity of seasonal rainfall leads to a large-scale regulation of water, in order to guarantee its supply to agriculture, as well as urban areas. This in turn, creates a situation where the coastal rainwater discharge is so reduced that many rivers are dry for seven to nine months out of the year.

As a consequence, the spreading of sediment on the coast is minimized, and the erosion process is accelerated on the beach, especially along the belts of the deltas, where the golf courses have been built. However, there are voices to the contrary of such a theory, such as that of the late, Dr. Derek Danta, former Dean of the School of Social and Behavioral Sciences, at California State University, Northridge and a

---

[57] *Ibid.*, 462-463
[58] *Ibid.*, 462-463
[59] *Ibid.*, 462-463

respected as well as renown American geographer, who, when questioned as to the validity of this premise, believed it to stand on unfounded grounds.

Some studies are intent on proving that the process of extracting sand from gravel, which is put to use in construction, combined with a continuous expansion of agriculture decimate, even to a greater extent the beach levels. By the same token, the fabrication of the marinas, along the coastline has provoked new movement of the beach sediment, allowing it to be dragged naturally to the reefs. The present stage of large-scale nutrition of the beaches is being used in order to recycle these materials.

There is an increasing awareness, as well as inevitably, a concern for the future of the environment of the Costa del Sol. This is captured in the national and regional directives established to reduce the tension existing between development and natural resources. The erosion of its beaches and its lack of water might suggest that the Costa del Sol is transitioning through the evolutionary phases of Butler's theory.

Lagiewski also includes Debbage (1990), as one of the pioneers in the analysis and application of the TALC to a tourism destination, upon demonstrating its validity, within the geographical framework of the Bahamas Islands in the Caribbean. This scholar argues that it is the oligopolistic nature of the region's market and not the fact that it has surpassed its visitor carrying capacity, with this tourism space, which has led to its entry into the decline phase. Thus, Debbage, himself indicates the following:

> One major trend in the organization of the tourist industry is the increasingly oligopolistic position of the primary tourist suppliers in the airline, hotel, tour operation, and travel agency sectors (and now, of course, the internet is, perhaps, the largest supplier, as indicated by López López, and de Esteban Curiel).[60]

And he continues:

> For resort destinations that depend on a small number of major suppliers for the bulk of the tourist product, it is likely that fluctuations, in the resort cycle will be just as influenced by the corporate strategies of a few key firms as it is by more localized concerns.[61]

Debbage's theory and the capacity of self-correction, which the system itself contains, as a function of a more sustainable tourism, appear encapsulated in the following quote by López López: "At the request of the Program of the United Nations for the Environment (PUNE), and in collaboration with the UNESCO, and the WOT the initiative was presented in Berlin, at the beginning of March 2000, by tour operators, that is to say, the business sector for a sustainable tourism."[62]

And he continues:

---

[60] Keith Debbage "Tourist Destination Cycles and Sustainable Development: A Comparative Analysis of the Bahamas and Mauritius," *Annals of the Tourism Research*, no. 17, (1990): 525.

[61] *Ibid.,*525

[62] Alejandro López López, "Desarrollo Sostenible: Medioambiente y turismo en las ciudades históricas: El caso de Toledo," *Observatorio Medioambiental*, no. 8 (2005): 337.

This represents a voluntary initiative, open to all tour operators, who intend to apply better practices, in the management of the environment, based on the exchange of information and experiences, the implementation of new technologies, the execution of assessments, including the collaboration with governments, the tourism industry and other entities.[63]

Lagiewski presents the case of Cyprus, as an example of interesting tourism development, as it applies to the Mediterranean, just as to the Costa del Sol. In the study Ioannides (1992) performs, he brings to light the role of this island's government, and the one played by multinational companies, in the change of the destination, throughout its evolution as a tourist destination. Cyprus' historical data proves that this tourism area followed the stages of exploration, participation and development. During these earlier stages, the government played an important role in the development of this industry.

Here, parallelisms may be drawn with the Costa del Sol and the facilities offered by the Franco regime for tourism development as a source of foreign currency. In the case of Cyprus, as in Spain, awareness existed, with regard to the tourism industry, in that it should be developed and used as a means to increase the entry of foreign currency and thus, in turn, diversify the economy. With this aim, the government-initiated efforts to stimulate the growth of the sector, through economic incentives and programs of loans for the development of the industry.

By the same token, in Cyprus, the Cyprus Tourism Organization was created, and, in Spain, the Ministry of Information and Tourism was established, in order to supervise the development of the sector. In Spain, this organization, as its name implies, devoted major resources to the global dissemination of the existence of this coastline. Propitiously, these governments also launched into the projects of building conveniently located airports and roads as arteries to transport the increasingly growing, as well as demanding tourist population.

During the stage of development, the Cypriot government was the driving force behind the recuperation of its tourist industry from the War of 1974. This was accomplished through the Emergency Plans of Action, in which an enormous priority was placed on tourism. The government also sponsored Plans of Action, at the end of the decade of the 70's, which provided economic incentives, such as loans at very low interest rates, free government giveaways of land to private investment companies, all with the purpose of making Cyprus into an international tourist destination.

Besides identifying the influence of the government in the TALC, Ionnides, in his study, also touches upon the role tour operators play in this theory. The influence of foreign tour operators, primarily, from countries, such as Great Britain, Germany and Sweden support Debagge's theory (1990), that these important suppliers played a significant role in the TALC.

In the case of Cyprus and also in the Costa del Sol, and other Spanish tourism localities this can be underscored specifically, by the importance the impact of charter flights had, as well as the appeal of tours designed especially for low budget travelers.

---

[63] *Ibid.*, pp.337

This bracket of low expenditure consumers led to establishment of buffet (especially breakfasts) in the hotels.

These factors are considered to be forces, which caused a negative interrelationship, with the environmental resources of the island, as well as cultural discrepancies. The same condition occurs, in the Costa del Sol, where commitments recently have been made, in order to attract a more affluent type of tourism. The dependence of Cyprus on a few tour operators has left an undeniable imprint on the island. The same has happened with the Spanish Costa del Sol, abandoning both spaces to their fate, in less competitive places, in the international market.

While Ioannides (1992) recognizes the increasing power that foreign tour operators have exerted on the island, does align itself with Butler's premise that this situation will increase throughout the tourism area life cycle, he does not, however, believe in its victimization. The government's interventionism implied a catharsis in tourism development. The government was able to react and see to it that the island would and could bounce back from the negative impacts of this industry on the island. Specifically, in the case of Cyprus, the government established measures for the tourism growth rate. In this way, upon creating equilibrium with the development of accommodation, he concludes that:

> ...the Cypriot government has intentionally steered the island's resort cycle towards Butler's 'consolidation stage'. Planners hope that through regulating the industry's growth and diversifying its nature, they will be able to protect its competitive ability, subsequently, forestalling the stagnation and decline.[64]

For Ioannides, also:

> Over the last three decades, the Cypriot government was and continues to be an important driving force of the tourism industry, first through purely economic growth strategies and later on through policies addressing socioeconomic issues and, increasingly, land-use and environmental concerns associated with this sector. Foreign presence in the accommodation sector has been minimal, unlike the case in some Caribbean destinations.[65]

He continues:

> Nevertheless, in recent years, external influence has become more evident with the increased activity of foreign tour operators and charter companies and the parallel loss of national airline's market share. This phenomenon reflects the increasing exogenous involvement in tourism, which Butler (1980) envisions for the development stage of the resort cycle.[66]

---

[64] Dimitri Ioannides, "Tourism Development Agents: The Cypriot Resort Cycle," *Annals of Tourism Research 19*, no. 4 (1992): 727.

[65] *Ibid.*, 727

[66] *Ibid.*, 727

That is to say, that in spite of the intervention of the government to coordinate the development of the industry, as in the case of Spain, there still continue to be negative spatial effects, both in the social and environmental order. The Cyprian coast has become a jungle of concrete apartment buildings, wherein the local and picturesque nature of the area has been lost.

Also, and as in the case of the Costa del Sol, the Doxey's previously mentioned "irredex" effect has overcome the population. Ioannides relates a similar occurrence, in one of his case studies, which took place in a village called Ayia. Here, its residents were so disgruntled by the pernicious presence of the "sun lusting" tourists that the population abandoned the town, seeking out a space away from these scantily clad individuals, who possessed a code of moral and ethics unshared and incomprehensible to the natives.

Upon establishing parallelisms between cases, such as the Spanish Costa del Sol and Cyprus, this study intends to prove that both private enterprise and the national, regional and municipal governments have led the tourism sector to the brink of stagnation, that is, to a situation of pre-stagnation. The unadulterated cultural and natural attractions are being substituted for other artificial ones, such as golf courses. This creates a limbo-like situation of "placelessness," in which the unique qualities of the tourism destination vanish and become a combined global grey zone.

Lagiewski mentions Sheela Argawal in two of her articles, which appeared in 1994 and 2001. She differs in her analysis of the final phases of the TALC and supports Hovinen in suggesting that the last stages of the TALC deserve modification. Her subject matter concerns the post-stagnation, specifically, the period of decline. In her first article, this scholar argues that the complete and absolute decline of a tourism destination is likely unacceptable, both politically and economically. Therefore, she proposes a phase of "reorientation," in which the destination will be observed making constant efforts to adjust to the changes before the decline occurs. Quite possibly, this theory may reveal a more positive and, perhaps, a more realistic slant on the organic life of a tourist destination.

This phase of reorientation may be applied to the Costa del Sol, in the eagerness of both private and public initiatives to stimulate the attractions of the place, with the implementation of the already mentioned golf courses, marinas, tennis facilities, spas, sports installations, equestrian centers, as well as cultural and historical attractions, such as the renowned Andalusian "White Villages." Notably, there also exists a delicious opportunity to explore the region's enticing gastronomic delicacies.

The tourist season has been extended thanks to this reorientation, which has produced both a quantitative, as well as a qualitative increase in the goods and services of the tourism industry. At the same time, public initiatives are being created, in order to prevent and control the deterioration of the region due to the impact of the tourist industry.

According to Lawieski, Agarwal (2002) integrates Butler's theory with the "restructuring" theory, upon intending to relate the causes and the consequences of the decline of a tourist destination. In her restructuring theory, she refers to the process of change in capitalistic societies and economies, which are, of course, already the majority of the globe. Agarwal also refers to significant changes in the strategies, by which capital seeks to accumulate. In this way, the researcher defines the restructuring according to the following terms:

> The core of the restructuring thesis concerns the analysis of the processes and strategies through which capital seeks expanded accumulation. Early research on restructuring has focused on the ways in which the primary and manufacturing industries have responded to increasingly competitive and to changing patterns of consumption. (Argietta 1979; Piore and Sabel 1984)[67]

Here, Agarwal includes a discussion on how industries respond to consumption and competition challenges. This is summarized into three main categories: the reorganization of the product, the reorganization of the labor force and the product transformation, and its new location on a spatial level. Afterwards, these strategies are defined according to the way, in which they relate to the "process of structural change" within the tourism context.

This researcher leaves the theoretical framework behind, as she enters the context of practice, by exploring the realities of three British coastal tourism destinations: Minehead, Weymouth and Scarborough. Each destination is characterized, by having entered the stage of post-stagnation. Agarwal maintains that when integrating the restructuring theory with the TALC, the possibilities of understanding and defining what the external factors are that play a role in the changes that occur in a tourist destination improve. The conclusion is drawn that here the decline, in most cases, is due to the result of the interaction between internal and external forces. Therefore, it is probable that, the responses to the decline are responses to external forces.

Agarwal concludes her article, by adding:

> This study demonstrates that there are theoretical relationships between the resort lifecycle and restructuring. In doing so, it highlights a number of important issues relating to the causes of decline and restructuring. First, decline is the outcome of internal and external forces; the latter intensifies the competitiveness of market conditions, while the former diminishes the competitiveness of the destination.[68]

She continues with her second and third consideration:

> Second, decline is an ongoing threat not necessarily associated with the course of the lifecycle or with a particular capitalist phase. Third,

---

[67] Sheela Agarwal, "Restructuring Seaside Tourism: The Resort Lifecycle," *Annals of Tourism Research* 29, no. 1 (2002): 28
[68] *Ibid.*, 48

restructuring is a continuous process which must be based on a greater appreciation of the uniqueness of the place.[69]

In her more recent study, which appeared in 2006, Argarwal arrives at similar conclusions, now, perhaps with a more futuristic slant:

> ...this paper discussed in-depth three key issues for future resort restructuring: first, that decline appears to be the outcome of interaction between internal and external forces of change; second, the threat of decline is not necessarily associated with the course of the TALC model or with a particular capitalist phase; and third restructuring is continuous and most involve attempts that recapture the uniqueness of resorts.[70]

Her thoughts follow accordingly:

> In doing so, this discussion has highlighted a number of future research avenues that relate broadly to the need to understand the role of these destinations in the global market-place, the nature, extent and success of local interaction with global forces of change, reasons for resort differential performance, the appropriateness of restructuring strategies ...[71]

And finally: ."..the most effective mechanisms that encourage cooperation and collaboration between the public and private sector."[72]

Agarwal observes that the degree of restructuring may affect the level of government intervention and that varies greatly from country to country, or from region to region. As has already been explored in Ioannides' study, it can be seen that the authority of the state has much to do with the development of the character of the destination.

She also arrives at the conclusion that both the application of the thesis of restructuring, as well as that of the TALC to a tourist destination contribute to the formulation of its response to a situation of decline. They may serve as an explanation to the causes and consequences of this condition. Without a doubt, these tools of analysis, when applied to the Costa del Sol, would be very useful, in order for this region to enter into the phase this scientist's terms as that of "reorientation."

FINAL CONSIDERATIONS

In summary, what remains to be a proven premise is that Butler's TALC theory can be transformed as a function of different tourism spaces in many ways. A greater

---

[69] *Ibid.*, 48
[70] Sheela Agarwal, "Coastal Resort Restructuring and the TALC," *The Tourism Area Life Cycle, Vol. 2, Conceptual and Theoretical Issues*, Butler RW. Ed. (Clevedon: Channel View Publications, 2006), 201-230
[71] *Ibid.*, 218
[72] *Ibid.*, 218

differentiation may be made of its phases or a new structure of its stages may be created. This is the pursuit of this study, when introducing the newly created stage of "pre-stagnation" to be applied to the Costa del Sol and, perhaps fittingly, to other tourism destinations as well.

Also, Butler's TALC theory may be combined in its application with other theories, as demonstrated by Agarwal, when joining it with the restructuring theory. Its units of analysis may be modified, as formulated, by many experts.

Whether this model is modified or not, it most certainly serves as a tool of approximation, in order to obtain a better understanding of the birth, growth or decay of the organic life of a tourism area. Within this rational and comprehensive framework of the TALC the destination is, so rightly, considered to be a vital space, which evolves as would any other living entity.

CHAPTER 4

Sustainable Tourism

ITS CONCEPT AND DEFINITIONS

Alejandro López López notably emphasizes that it was during the beginning of the decade of the '70s that new approaches regarding the subject of tourism appeared from critical and environmental perspectives. To this end, this scientist is ahead of his time, with the following definition regarding sustainable tourism:

> it implies the ability to maximize net benefits of the economic development, subject to the maintenance of services and the quality of natural resources, throughout time. The economic development is interpreted, in a broad sense, to include, not only the increase of real per capita income, but, also, other elements of social welfare. The development would include a structural change in the economy and in the society. [73]

López López continues: "The maintenance of services, and the quality of the endowment of resources throughout time, implies, to the degree that it is possible, the acceptance of the following rules:"[74]

He follows by citing them:

> a) "The utilization of renewable natural resources at a lesser pace or equal to its rhythm of natural replenishment.
> b) The maximization of the use of non-renewable resources, subject to the substitution of resources and technological progress."[75]

Following this same line of thought, the journal *Annals of Tourism Research* deals with such issues as the psychology of the tourist, the role of leisure in the urban industrialized society, the symbolism of vacationing, and even its first expectations for the environment. This journal, without a doubt, was at the cutting edge of the movement, which arose subsequently to that of sustainable tourism. However, López López and de Esteban Curiel, uncover the primary form of the definition, upon summarizing theirs in the following terms:

---

[73] *Op. Cit,.* López López, 333
[74] *Ibid.,* 334.
[75] *Ibid.,* 334.

Sustainable development has been defined as a pattern of types of socio-economical structural transformations, which optimize the social and economic benefits of the present, without risking the potential of obtaining similar benefits in the future. Therefore, sustainable tourism is any and every type of tourism (whether it is based on natural resources or not), which contributes to sustainable development.[76]

Before defining such a theoretical and practical body, it is worth underlining that the concept of sustainable tourism arises as a response to traces of decadence in the ecological, as well as cultural and sociological environment, which have been sacrificed because of economic motivations. There are various definitions of sustainable tourism, which are used within the realm of this study. Richard Butler defines it in 1993, but it had not been considered a tourism element, which was accomplished through the Asymmetric Digital Subscriber Line, also known as the ADSL, or the Internet. According to López López and Javier de Esteban Curiel (2008), this means of travel is:

In spite of representing a form of mass consumption, it is environmentally sustainable. There is no travel, and, therefore, no negative impact. Socially, it creates qualified technological employment. Economically, it contributes to the development of tourist activity in the society of knowledge, and in this way, to the growth of the PIB. [77]

Also, according to these scientists, this type of tourism is especially beneficial for mature destinations. However, digressing still, it may be necessary to specify the very definition of tourism. In the state of California, in which most of the southern portion of this state's climate is considered to be Mediterranean, Sam Farr, a California congressman, who served, from 1993 to 2017, when he retired after the 2016 elections, speaks about this industry in one of his speeches:

Tourism is America's largest industry. It employs 19 million people in each and every congressional district and territory. California is a state of 33 million people, and long ago the state realized if they could just get 33 million people to get out of their house and move about 40 miles a day, and that is what the definition of a tourist is...[78]

[76] Alejandro López López et al., "Turismo , internet e indicadores ambientales de sostenibilidad," *Observatorio Medioambiental*, no. 11 (2008): 198.

[77] *Ibid.*, 187

[78] U.S Congress House Committee on International Relations. Subcommittee on Travel and Tourism Partnership Act: *Joint Hearing Before International Economic Policy and Trade*. (Washington: House of Representatives, One Hundred Fourth Congress).

The congressman continues with the definition of a tourist as: "…somebody who is 40 miles away from home, then dependent on local restaurants or dependent on another gas station, or whatever, then you can really stimulate the economy."[79]

Tourism has even been considered to be the largest global industry. This basic definition of a person who leaves his or her house and simply travels 40 miles without all of the additions to a classical vacation, such as plane travel to a destination, a more or less expensive hotel stay, including meals at restaurants *in situ* confirm this fact.

However, in order to fully meet the criterion of this definition, it is necessary for oil prices to maintain a steady low. These have varied during the first two decades. They have been as high as almost $150 per barrel in 2008 and have slumped to a rock-bottom price of below $40 at the beginning of 2016. The prices are still relatively low, at nearly $60 a barrel by the end of 2017, and still on the rise by the end of 2018.

These prices are not reflected at the pump, however. The price American consumers pay for gas seems to constantly maintain an artificial high. California, at the time this study was written, reflects the highest price in all of the states in the continental United States. However, these high prices are not reflected in the traffic of the cities, or freeways, as the residents of this state continue to battle congested conditions, day or night, amid rush-hour or not.

Although, gas consumption would stimulate and develop the economy, perhaps a better approach to a more maintainable tourism industry, based on a sustainable economy, would be to create and invest in alternative sources of energy, such as wind or solar. Electrical cars, such as Tesla or the Chevrolet Volt, to mention a few, are seen more and more on the freeways. Also, cars that run on solar and only water or oxygen are being developed. All of these would decrease the CO_2 emissions and, thus, benefit the environment in the prevention of climate change.

However, López López and de Esteban Curiel indicate in their study (2008) that the stable price of fuel has been precisely one of the main factors in keeping with the tourism expansion. They say:

> The Spanish tourism supply has been mainly directed to a mid to low level spending class, which conforms to the phenomenon of "sun and beach tourism, characterized by massification. This growth in tourism has, also, benefited from the ease of travel (such as, for the example, the changes which are being made in low-cost airlines, which diversify the offer to a greater tourist population), and because of the stability of fuel prices since the 1970's (Ministry of the Environment, 2006). [80]

At the same time, it has been proven and said that the existence of tourism on the planet is necessary to sustain its ecology, as well as other social, cultural and economic activities. López López states the requirements of tourism development:

---

[79] Ibid.
[80] Ibid., 192

To this end, all nations are required to pursue a type of development, which integrates the production, with the conservation, and increase of resources, and which joins and makes available to all, a convenient means of existence with equal access to all resources. [81]

It is understood that these resources may include alternative energy sources, which do not harm the environment, as well as renewable resources, such as water, which is a very precious asset in areas such as the Costa del Sol. This is, in great measure, due to the consumption of drinking water by the golf courses, and their lack of usage of recycled water for their needs. It is also necessary to mention within this category the ecological resources of flora and fauna, which are native to this region and may be on the brink of suffering extinction.

López López continues with his definition of sustainable development:

The concept of sustainable development provides the structure in which the environmental policies, as well as strategies for development may be integrated, using the term "development," in its broadest sense. Sustainable development tries to satisfy the needs and aspirations of the present without compromising those of the future. [82]

He also recognizes: "Without, in the least, desiring to slow down economic growth, it is understood that the problems of underdevelopment and poverty cannot be resolved, unless a new era of growth is established."[83]

This quote values the capacity of tourism as a primary force in development and the antithesis of poverty, as long as its fundamental resources are not abused. Therefore, it is understood that what is harvested in the present are as important as those assets, which can be harvested in the future. Of course, all of this depends on the policies and strategies, which are applied to the environment.

On the other hand, he continues:

One of the recent proposals in relation to sustainable development has been that of Jiménez Herrero (1989), which includes critical elements of sustainable cooperation. Here, it is affirmed that the framework of cooperation, in support of global sustainability is conditioned by the consequences of the "inaction," or not acting now, would mean greater costs of imbalance for the future—and because of the current system of international economic relations which continued to be rooted in a system of domination/dependency. [84]

In fact, the postponement of the practice of sustainable tourism causes its negative consequences to fall irremediably on the backs of the international community. This

---

[81] Op. Cit., López López, 334
[82] *Ibid.*, 334
[83] *Ibid.*, 334
[84] *Ibid.*, 335

lack of responsibility, as well as the ability to act, will notoriously empty on to the realities of developing countries, as opposed to those that are developing or underdeveloped. It is precisely the former that must take up the role of leadership, when formulating tourism policies, which favor the ecological environment, and the cultural and social activities, as well as economic relations.

López López continues with certitude:

> Due to reasons of global security----both in terms of the economic, as well as ecological realms---a remodeling of the ground rules of a symmetrical relationship North/South, which allows for a more equal incorporation, of the peripheral economies to become integrated into the global economic system with products of improved quality, greater added value, less consumption of energy, and less environmental impact.[85]

In this way, an example can be made of the golf courses in the Spanish Costa de Sol, as a case of an entity, which causes great impact to the environment. This is caused, in the first instance, by their great consumption of the scarce but renewable resource, water, and then continues with their usage of chemicals such as fertilizers, which includes, but does not conclude, with the destruction these manmade installations cause to the native and regional flora and fauna.

To this end, López López and de Esteban Curiel speak to the fragility of natural spaces, in which the otherwise known as the Spanish Costa del Golf, may be included:

> The pressure that tourism exercises on natural spaces is a reason for concern due to the possible alteration of its characteristics. The high ecological value and the fragility of these spaces make them even more vulnerable to the tourist activity developed, in the majority of cases, in the form of daily visits, and controlled over-night stays.[86]

And they continue, along these same lines with the following: "Because of this, the Public Administration provides for a system of zoning for the National Parks according to the fragility of their surrounding and various plans and programs for the management of the public use of these spaces." [87]

With the same intent, a management policy could be implemented to organize with a similar function the natural surroundings of and those contained there within the golf courses. It could also be analyzed, which, of course, would be the subject matter of a very different research project, if the impact created by the golf courses on the environment is compensated by this new economic tourist activity.

In the majority of cases, these sporting courses are found in what had been farmland, historically used for agriculture, where the preferred crop had been potatoes and green peppers. A study would have to be made, as to whether, this previous

---

[85] Ibid., 335
[86] *Op. Cit.* Alejandro López López, et al., 194
[87] *Ibid.,* 194

agricultural activity yielded more profit than golf or vice-versa. López López and de Esteban Curiel continue to expound, on this subject:

> The growth of sustainable job creation, throughout the years, as well as the arrival of the number of foreign tourists, however does not go hand in hand with a greater economic growth of the sector. The objective consists in increasing job creation, as well as the economic derivatives from tourism, while, at the same time, preserving the natural resources of the area's visited, and avoiding their massification by tourism.[88]

Therefore, it can be observed that the benefits of tourism are not always clear, or transparent. In terms of another subject, that is, the sustainable resources of a city, López López has the following opinion:

> Within the tourism resources of each city, the historical heritage is susceptible to taking on a primary or secondary position, as a function of its capacity to attract visitors. In other words, not all nuclei of Collective History are created equally. Therefore, the large metropolitan conglomerations present a complex dominant profile, with a strong presence of business tourism and different modalities of cultural tourism.[89]

López López continues:

> The historical heritage plays a secondary role, in any case, it does not constitute the main attraction for visitors. In the coastal sites, something similar happens. Even though cities such as San Sebastián, Cádiz and La Coruña count on a considerable amount of historical heritage, their tourism character is associated with their endowment of natural resources, in particular, their beaches.[90]

Along these same lines, this expert, in the field, writes:

> In the final analysis, there are a number of towns and villages whose cultural heritage does not attract a significant amount of tourism. It can even be said that the majority of such nuclei lack sufficient attraction, on their own, to generate a relevant pull into each one's respective areas: their attraction derives from their insertion within a larger tourism scale, which is a wider tourism area, with more heterogeneous resources.[91]

López López's theory may be confirmed and associated with that of Paolo Antonio Russo (2006), related to Venice, and entitled the theory of the "Vicious Cycle." As

---

[88] Ibid., 196
[89] Op. Cit., Alejandro López López, 339.
[90] Ibid., 339
[91] Ibid., 339

has been stated in another section of this study and following the guidelines of these two scientists, it is the historical urban center, which contains the magnetic pull for the rest of the tourist activity of the region.

However, in the case of the Spanish Costa del Sol, it may be concluded, along with López López's theory, that its "tourism profile" is related to the area's natural endowments of beaches and, more recently, golf courses. The latter has taken over this space to such a degree that it is now called, with familiarity, the Costa del Golf, due to their overriding physical presence, as well as their exhausting capability, to drain the precious water resources of the area.

López López also considers the plight of the mature tourist destination the category, in which the Costa del Sol falls:

> In a general context of growth of tourism demand, the historical cities, in as much as they are an ecosystem, based upon heritage, face the challenge of responsible and sustainable management, in activities related to leisure and tourism. Just as in the case of natural spaces, tourism, which occurs, in a city, is not innocuous. In fact, the high influx of visitors is beginning to present environmental problems of tourism saturation, concentrated both temporally and spatially in the, so called, 'mature' destinations.[92]

The Costa del Sol is also a mature tourism destination, although it is composed by a series of small urban centers. As has been previously mentioned, it may be said that the golf courses, which are being built, along with their adjoining, housing developments, hotels, and restaurants are becoming autonomous and independently functioning nuclei, which distract the tourism activity, with its subsequent economic activity, from the mature beach towns.

These golf courses, with all of their adjacent structures, may be considered as what Russo denominated to be studied in another chapter of this book, "the contentious tourism spaces." That is to say, they take away natural resources, such as water, from the original mature center, as well as its economic activity and welfare.

López López speaks to the concept of "carrying capacity," when applied to these historical sites:

> The dimensions of the tourism carrying capacity may constitute the necessary environmental requirements for historical cities. Therefore, whatever may be used as the point of departure, in order to define the concept of tourism carrying capacity, this, always, implicitly contains the idea of restriction or limit, beyond which the 'tourism' exploitation of a particular resource is unsustainable because of the harm it may cause.[93]

This scientist continues to point out that:

---

[92] Ibid., 339
[93] *Ibid.* pp. 340

The nature of this limit, be it physical, perceptual or economical, make it possible to allow for the contemplation of different dimensions, at the time of determining the carrying capacity of a space. Therefore, it may be termed as a physical carrying capacity, ecological carrying capacity, social carrying capacity (from the standpoint of the visitors), anthropological carrying capacity (from the standpoint of the residents, economical carrying capacity, etc.[94]

Even though the Costa del Sol is not a historic city, in the following section of this book, the intent is to prove that the golf courses with all their structural accessories represent contentious spaces with various urban nuclei of beach tourism. The golf courses, which are exemplary of such spaces, create "physical limits," in using López López's terminology in the area, upon so exhaustively consuming the scarce water resources. This action is causing a reaction in certain sectors of the Andalusian population, that is to say, his term, the "anthropological perception," which encapsulates how "the standpoint of the resident" is summarized in a rejection of this ecological burden that, in this way, has been placed upon the region.

In the same article, the author continues to explain the dimensions, as well as the facets of tourism exploitation:

The denomination and classification of these dimensions vary from one author to the next as a function of their background, and the spatial realm, in which, they have centered their analysis. However, essentially, they, fundamentally, make reference to the four types of factors, which affect the tourism subsystem...[95]

Therefore, in this way, in the Costa del Sol, it is the physical factors, and the role they play, in the environment, mainly, regarding the consumption of water, this renewable but highly scarce resource, in the region. This, in turn, affects the social factors, which modify to a negative point in some sectors the reaction to the presence of visitors. These impact the environment, creating Russo's "contentious space," which takes away from the benefit of the urban nuclei of beaches.

López López continues: "At the urban level, that is to say, in more diversified spaces where the tourism function inserts itself in a more complex economic reality, the concept of carrying capacity can be considered a network of intermingling realities."[96]

The author describes what these are:

Some may fit the framework of the so called quantifiable objective dimensions, others, however, must be approached from more subjective and qualitative perspectives. Therefore, tourism carrying capacity (ecological, physical, and economical), more qualitative perspectives linked to the

---

[94] *Ibid.* pp. 340
[95] *Ibid.*, 340
[96] *Ibid.*, 340

interrelationships between the local-visiting populations, and the political, as well as decisive actions of local management, may be outlined.[97]

Even though the Spanish Costa del Sol is not an urban tourism destination, very similar criterions, as the ones mentioned in the previous cite, may be applied to it. The carrying capacity in this region should also be subjective and qualitative, as well as quantitative, given the fact that the relationship of visitors/residents, with the latter's impact on the environment, is causing the former's attitude to vary toward this group in a negative way.

López López mentions six elements, which vary in time and space in the scope of tourism. They are:

1. The ecological dimension.
2. The physical dimension.
3. The economic dimension.
4. The local residents' perspective.
5. The visitors' perspective.
6. The political dimension.

It may be affirmed, at the same time, that these six aspects are, dialectically, interrelated. The first element is the tourist and the natural environment. The second aspect is that of the infrastructures created by the society, visited by the tourist.

López López categorizes the economical dimension of a tourist destination when he describes its configuration, when the following adjustments occur spatially: "the greatest benefit of tourism exploitation (much greater than any of the other urban functions), displaces those of lesser value, from the center to more peripheral locations."[98]

Thus, a "contentious space," a term created by Antonio Paolo Russo and, which is discussed in the following chapter, is created.

The visitor's perspective and that of the residents are completely intertwined and interdependent, as the satisfaction of one depends upon the satisfaction of the other. Rarely in society, is such a symbiotic relationship so apparent between two coexisting communities of interests.

The political dimension, however, according to Alejandro López López is the element, which must establish the dialectical hierarchy between these social components. In his view, it must directly coordinate the management of the tourism industry, for the benefit of both parties, without self-serving or personal profiteering.

However, as it has been proven, on so many occasions, both globally and specifically, on the Costa del Sol, the functions of the different municipalities, those of the Autonomous Region, as well as the role of the Central State, have served primarily to benefit only a few. In turn, the well-being of the majority has been sacrificed.

---

[97] *Ibid.*, 340
[98] Ibid., 341

It can be said, that these aspects, mentioned by this scientist, can be applied to all types of tourism destinations; that is to say, those which are consistently urban – the urban/historical type, as might be the case of Toledo in Spain or Venice, which are dealt with in this book. Other types of tourism to be considered upon applying these categories would be rural tourism and, finally, sun and sand tourism or urban tourism, which is encompassed by the Spanish Costa del Sol.

The importance of sustainable tourism, in all its aspects, is reflected in López López's following quote, which reflects clear optimism but, at the same time, is tinged with caution: "Tourism has become a very important reason to conserve the environment, there are those who even believe, perhaps with exaggeration, that the only spaces that will be saved from environmental degradation are those which have some touristic tourism value."[99]

Alejandro López López continues with his thoughts on the importance of sustainable tourism: "In any case, what is evident is that nature tourism has great economic potential for local sustainable development and it also offers an excellent opportunity for educational environmental projects."[100]

He adds, with caution: "However, it is also evident that tourism generates a series of problems and limitations, which should not be ignored, when strategic planning of tourism development is put into place in a protected natural space."[101]

López López expresses the underlying idea that tourism responds to a need to care for, as well as conserve, the environment when he says:

> In summary, we find that the new tourism demand is more and more sensitive to environmental problems. This is reflected in changes in the behavior of the tourists in recent years. On one hand, there is a perception of a more responsible attitude towards the maintenance of their place of vacation.[102]

He continues:

> "On the other, a tendency to travel, independently, is observed, which, usually is accompanied by a greater respect for local traditions and customs. There is a taste and a demand for unique forms of lodging, even with lesser levels of comfort, but always with the protection of the natural milieu, the cultural heritage and environment, in general, by the tourist destination"[103]

Now to continue with the tourist area of Lancaster County in the state of Pennsylvania, inhabited primarily by the religious/cultural group of the Amish. This county has an ample history, which dates back to the 18th century, when the first American

---

[99] Alejandro López López, "El medio ambiente y las nuevas tendencias turísticas: referencia a la región de Extremadura," *Observatorio Medioambiental* , 4 (2001): 212
[100] *Ibid.,* 212
[101] *Ibid.,* 212
[102] *Ibid.,* 212
[103] *Ibid.,* 212-213

Continental Congress took place there, and therefore maintains the distinction of having been the capital of the U.S. for one day.

Also, this location, aside from being a cultural and spiritual settlement, given the well-known fact that the Amish reject any type of technological advancement, they continue to live in the context of that remote past. Thus, it has become a renowned tourist destination, which offers a very varied historical, cultural, as well as religious and commercial product. Also, agricultural tourism has been introduced, as well as gastronomical, with its famous and much sought after "shoofly" cake, along with their specially crafted pretzels.

Gary R. Hovinen, who has very carefully studied this tourist destination, refers to sustainable tourism when he writes:

> ...The tourism sector is related to and dependent upon other sectors of the economy and society, so any definition of sustainable tourism must consider the overall system and not simply tourism alone. The difficulty of implementing sustainable tourism, therefore, becomes apparent.[104]

And he finishes with the following thought: "Perhaps it is best to view sustainable tourism as a set of idealistic principles that may be useful as a basis for long-range planning rather than a condition ever likely to be fully achieved."[105]

Therefore, this scientist maintains that there must be a clear equilibrium, between economic, ecological and social needs, in order for there to exist sustainable tourism, in his region of study:

> The first consideration of sustainable tourism principles in Lancaster County occurred as part of the preparation of the 1998 Heritage Tourism Plan. A basic premise of the heritage tourism program was that there is a need to maintain a strong balance between the economic benefits of tourism, and the preservation of natural and cultural resources.[106]

This Historical Tourism Plan was composed of the following points, which are worth citing, as their particular validity lead to an all-encompassing certainty:

1) The natural and cultural environment has intrinsic value, and its protection and preservation is (sic) essential to the long-term success and viability of tourism in Lancaster County.
2) The relationship between tourism and the environment, both natural and cultural, must be managed so that it is sustainable in the long term.[107]

---

[104] Gary Hovinen, "Lancaster County the TALC, and the Search for Sustainable Tourism," in *The Tourism Area Life Cycle Vol 1, Applications and Modifications* Butler, RW (ed), (Clevedon: Channel View Publications, 2006): 80
[105] *Ibid.*, 80.
[106] *Ibid.*, 80.
[107] *Ibid.* pp. 80-81.

3) Tourism should enhance and complement the unique natural cultural features of Lancaster County.

4) Tourism activities should respect and accurately reflect the scale, nature, and character of Lancaster County's unique places.[108]

The following ideas on carrying capacity are mentioned:

5) Carrying capacity should be a prime consideration in managing and protecting the natural and cultural heritage of Lancaster County.

6) A balance should be sought between the needs of the visitor, the place, and the residents of Lancaster County.[109]

Hovinen finalizes with these points, regarding sustainable and sensitive tourism:

7) Tourism should communicate appropriate cultural and environmental sensitivity.

8) Local involvement in sustainable tourism planning processes is essential in promoting harmony between tourism and the residents of Lancaster County. (Lancaster County Planning Commission, 1998).

Hovinen continues, with this opinion: "In order for a tourism destination to remain competitive and thereby to support the goal of achieving sustainable tourism, the tourism industry should emphasize unique attractions rather than relying mainly on standardized and 'artificial' attractions imported from the outside."[110]

He follows with this description of Lancaster County:

One long-term strength of the county has been the unique Amish population and their distinctive culture. But to sustain tourism at a high level of visitation it is necessary to develop additional unique attractions. This has been one of the Lancaster/County heritage tourism program since its inception in the mid-1990's.[111]

The Spanish Costa del Sol does follow Hovinen's theory, in that it depends too greatly on the imported and artificial tourism resources of the Costa del Sol. Its intensively and extensively developed sports structures convert this region into a form of "placelessness," where it loses its uniqueness, while converting it into an area similar to any place on the globe.

These spaces become spatially distorted. The golfers/tourists lodge themselves in resorts, where there is no need to stray from the comfortable but limiting design of their areas. From their vantage point, it is not necessary to explore the towns and

---

[108] Ibid. pp. 80-81.
[109] *Ibid.,* 80-81.
[110] *Ibid.,* 85
[111] *Ibid.,* 85

villages of the region itself. The region's unique culture, such as the delicious Andalusian gastronomy, as well as its rare architecture, welcoming beaches and cozy coves.

When applying Butler's original theory to Lancaster County, Hovinen bases himself on it when saying:

> Earlier stages of exploration, involvement, and development with many of the characteristics suggested by Butler in his 1980 formulation are clearly discernable. But the county tourism industry is now mature, and highly diversified, and problems arise when trying to fit the tourism trends of the past quarter century to Butler's assumptions of a progression to later stages of consolidation, stagnation, and then either possible decline or complete rejuvenation.[112]

This scientist believes that there is a combination of phases in the stage of mature tourism, which influence its development. To this end, he writes:

> "In the diversified and essentially culturally based tourism destination of Lancaster County, different sectors of tourism (older versus newer attractions, variety of accommodations, shopping alternatives, chain versus local restaurants) have combined to create what is now a mature industry where growth, stagnation, decline, and revitalization through reinvestment or new investment coexist."[113]

And Hovinen continues:

> "One tourism sector, or a portion of a sector, may have results in a given year that contrast with those of another sector. The different elements of tourism can be said to have their own individual life cycles. Some individual businesses thrive in a given year while others stagnate or even decline."[114]

To this end he points out:

> "An owner of an accommodations facility, for example reported to the author record results for the first six months of 2002 at the same time that some traditional attractions experienced stagnation (personal communication, August 2002). The overall industry may exhibit fluctuating growth patterns year to year based on a complex combination of internal and external factors"[115]

---

[112] *Ibid.*, 89
[113] Ibid., 89
[114] Ibid., 89
[115] *Ibid.*, 89

While citing the example of the characteristics of a mature stage of a tourism destination, Hovinen says:

> "A temporary decline may be followed by a growth spurt, as happened when the major attraction Sight and Sound was destroyed by fire and then rebuilt. A number of county tourism businesses apparently benefited in the first half of 2002 from the tendency of many Americans to prefer destinations that they could easily drive to in the new age of terrorism."[116]

Therefore, the idea may be drawn from the aforementioned statements, as well as Richard W. Butler's TALC model, which suggests a situation of complete decadence, when in reality, there may be a combination of stages in this phase of the cycle. Gary Hovinen points to the necessity of there being a long-term plan, in order to avoid the decadence of the tourism space. This may involve both the private, as well as the public sectors, operating in an association of municipalities, with the purpose of restructuring or reorienting this industry. Agarwal expresses similar ideas in her article, "Coastal Resort Restructuring and the TALC" (2002).

In order to further discuss the reality of sustainable tourism, such remote destinations as Thailand, may be explored, specifically the village of Karen, in the northern hills of this country. J. Marois and T. Hinch make the following comment, to this very meaningful point on sustainability: "Any discussion of the sustainability of tourism development in this village must, therefore, consider culture as the defining element."[117]

That is to say that the tourism industry of this small region depends on the existence of an indigenous culture, more so than the artificial draws, such as the Spanish Costa del Sol's golf courses, or other tourism product variants, which are based on the amusements of local beaches.

These authors state:

> "Two different types of tours emerged. The first was a *jungle trek* consisting of a guided trek into the forest to visit more remote and traditional hill tribe villages with few tourist facilities. These treks operate with an average of 10-12 participants and last three to ten days."[118]

The description continues:

> "The second type was a *tribal village* or *sightseeing tour* in which most of the transportation is by van, bus or boat. These tours travel through Northern Thailand, stopping at various villages for short 'picture opportunities'.

---

[116] *Ibid.*, Hovinen, 89
[117] M. Marois et al., "Seeking Sustainable Tourism in Northern Thailand: The Dynamics of the TALC," *The Tourism Area Life Cycle, Vol. 1 Applications and Modifications*, Richard W. Butler (ed.), (Clevedon: Channel View Publications, 2006), 250.
[118] *Ibid.*, 251.

Typically, sightseeing tours consist of relatively large groups of 20-40 people and last from one to three days."[119]

They end with the similarities of both types of tours:

"For both types of tours, the tour operator is responsible for the operational details including transportation, accommodation, food and luggage handling, thereby making these tours accessible to a wide range of visitors."[120]

If this tourism realm is related to the TALC, and to sustainable tourism, it is observed that the tourists who visit this region, are growing at an increasingly fast pace. This leads to the conclusive assumption that the cycles mentioned, in Butler's theory, are quickly traversed as well.

Therefore, it will be difficult to maintain a situation of sustainable tourism, as it has been defined, in this chapter, neither in terms of the near future or that of a more distant nature. It can be said, that this region, in relation to its short-lived existence, has been excessively dynamic and rapid in its growth to maintain any form of sustainability.

FINAL CONSIDERATIONS

A deeper analysis of this region may be made, which reveals the following:

"The hill tribe trekking product has progressed rapidly through its life cycle with a shift from the village (Ban Raummit) being a featured stop on the early trekking tours to it being an important staging point for treks to more isolated villages."[121]

Ban Raummit is described in the following terms:

"As the village was losing its appeal as a 'primitive' stop for trekking tours, it was gaining popularity as a major stop on sightseeing tours. Indicators suggest this sightseeing product is currently in a mid to advanced development stage."[122]

However, this development is coming at a cost to the village, as follows:

"Visitor demands are being met through increased tourism services and infrastructure. Yet, these vestiges of modernity have reduced its 'charm' as a

---

[119] *Ibid.*, 251
[120] *Ibid.*, 251
[121] *Ibid.*, 267
[122] *Ibid., 267*

relatively traditional village. Manifestations of modern life are undercutting Ban Raummit's appeal as a stop on sightseeing tours and accelerating its trajectory through the TALC."[123]

As was previously mentioned, the intent of this study has been to prove that the TALC theory may simplify the life of a tourist destination, upon defining so narrowly the life sequences of a space destined for such an end. It is possible, as has already been mentioned, that various cycles coexist at the same time in the area destined for tourism. In the village of Ban Raummit, a form of cultural tourism exists. This type of tourism is, perhaps, the one that most swiftly moves the place through the cycles qualified by Butler. This is due to the fact that the host population is very susceptible to modification by foreigners, when there is an interaction between them.

In the Costa del Sol, there has also been a cultural interference with the tourism industry, although the draw, which originates the displacement of tourism, has traditionally been the three S's; that is, "sea," "sun," and "sand," and now, of course, it also includes the sport of golf. To this end, it may be said that tourism has developed, within a specific ecological framework that is within the design, as well as furnished by the Mediterranean climate.

It is important to say that the authors of this article do not believe that the TALC is useful to determine a situation of sustainable tourism. To this end, they declare:

"The perplexing question of when life starts or finishes must be asked in the case of the TALC, just as it is asked in the case of human life cycles. The TALC offers a useful tool to track development, make decisions about the pace and nature of change in the present and to predict change in the future. It does not, however, allow, for definitive statements on sustainability."[124]

Leaving this subject in a state of unresolved disagreement at this time, it may be fitting to bring up the article, by Brian Wheeler (2006), in which this author applies, creatively, and to some observers, what may be a stretch of the imagination, the TALC to singer and performer, Elvis Presley, as a sustainable tourist product. Wheeler writes the following:

"Clearly, there are a number of ways Elvis, and the Elvis phenomenon, can be seen as a part of tourism and the tourist industry--- manifesting, most obviously, as a generator of tourism trips. "[125]

This author, creatively, continues:

---

[123] *Ibid.,* 267
[124] *Ibid.,* 268
[125] Brian Wheeler, "The King is Dead, Long Live the Product: Authenticity, Sustainability, and the Product Life Cycle," *The Tourism Area Life Cycle. Vol 1 Applications and Modifications* Butler, RW (ed.) (Clevedon: Channel View Publications, 2006), 339

"Evidenced in the pilgrimages to Graceland, to locations featured in his dubious backlog of films, even to Prestwick Airport in West Scotland, site of Elvis's only--- recent sightseeing apart---- visit to the UK, there can be no doubt that Elvis is big tourism business."[126]

Although, this view of a sustainable tourism product may seem unorthodox and irreverent, Wheeler maintains the logic of his article, by comparing Elvis Presley to an Amazonian jungle. He sustains that Elvis, in terms of a tourism product was: "...the wild animal that became the managed, domesticated, cultivated product. He metamorphosed from a feral wild cat—a hip, hep, hell cat—to the big, flabby, neutered pet pussy cat of his later years."[127]

He continues writing:

"His rise, decline --- from erotic to neurotic, demise and then subsequent rejuvenation (resurrection might be more apposite here) mirrors and serves as metaphor for, the well-researched phases of the resort cycle."[128]

Wheeler himself recognizes that he has assumed a poetic license, in order to compare the figure of Elvis Presley, as a man trapped in the urban jungle, to wild jungle animals. The author discerned this analogy during an ecotourism trip that he made to the Amazonian. There, he found parallelisms in the relationship between Elvis, ecotourism and tourism product sustainability, as well as the TALC theory.

It is interesting how Brian Wheeler makes spatial observations regarding the TALC, instead of the necessary, as well as obvious temporal ones. He finds that the eco-hotels, which are located on the shores of the Amazon River, and at a greater distance, from the city of Manaus, are more primitive. Those that are spatially nearer to this formerly glorious, rubber-producing hub and provincial capital offer material comforts, which are more similar to those available in the Western world. In this geographic region, the TALC is applied, but with qualitative considerations.

Therefore, attention is drawn to the Ariau Tower, which is located, approximately three hours, by boat, from Manaus. This is an example of an eco-hotel which offers all the modern comforts and where spoiled guests may enjoy, in a protected environment, a swimming pool, air conditioning, and even toilets with running water.

On the opposite side of the spectrum, the Reserva Natural Xixuau was found. This reserve, which barely qualifies as a hotel but serves, mainly, as shelter for the intrepid traveler, is located 40 hours from Manaus. Precisely here is where Wheeler's creative wheel begins to spin:

"Now superimpose on this profile Elvis's earthy life cycle, from youth to premature death at 42. The Xixuau Reserve then equates to the raw teen idol

[126] *Ibid.,* 339
[127] *Ibid.,* 340
[128] *Ibid.,* 340

circa 1956 and the Ariau Tower to the commodified, bloated, idle Elvis of later years"[129]

The analogy continues:

"Distanced from civilization, the wildness of the Xixuau Lodge---its primitive, unpretentious, no frills, natural authenticity---represents the unconstructed Elvis from the early days... But already there were problems. How to maintain and sustain the momentum of success?"[130]

The author explains with the following:

"Already the wheels had been set in motion. Elvis had moved from Sun Records to RCA, from specialist to mainstream; from small to mass market, from local to national to international. Molded to take full advantage of market opportunities, Elvis was stage managed." [131]

Elvis Presley had become domesticated and had transferred to another phase of the TALC, both in the temporal and qualitative sense, as opposed to the geographical destination of the Amazon, which fit into that of the qualitative spatial phase.

To a certain degree, both the development of the Amazon, as well as that of the "rock" icon Elvis Presley are tourist products. As such entities, both do or do not enjoy sustainability, depending upon the application of political management, be it at the macro or micro level.

In this chapter, various scientists have been quoted, who advocate political management, from the extreme view of Elvis Presley, whose case was the most doubtful and least altruistic, to the definition presented by Alejandro López López or that devised by Richard W. Butler himself. The latter, decidedly, believes that sustainable tourism is a dialectical product, in which social, cultural, economic and ecological activities must coexist under the prioritization of a neutral and disinterested general policy. This policy must balance the needs of each one of these elements, otherwise, if the presence of any of the above-mentioned aspects is exaggerated, this very delicate network of relationships will become unbalanced.

The social, as well as cultural activities are aware that if attention is not given to the environment, their economic well-being may be jeopardized. It becomes more and more obvious for capitalistic economic activities, if care is not given to the environment, no profit will be made in the actions of tourism, nor in any other tasks, in which this sector is involved.

---

[129] *Ibid.*, 342
[130] *Ibid.*, 342
[131] *Ibid.*, 342

CHAPTER 5

TALC in its Spatial Perspective: A Comparative Study of the Costa Del Sol and Venice

Using as a basis, two texts by Antonio Paolo Russo (2002, 2006), this chapter deals with the case of Venice, as was mentioned, in the Introduction. Here the intent is to determine, based, on their similarities, and differences, the condition of the Costa del Sol, as a mature tourism destination, in the new stage, defined in this book, as that of "pre-stagnation."

VENICE AND THE COSTA AS COMPARATIVE DESTINATIONS

Venice may be taken as an example of how a Mediterranean city or locality suffers from the consequences of tourism abuse and overuse, and then, results in both congestion of population, as well as that of infrastructures. This happens, in a similar manner, in the urban centers of the Spanish Costa del Sol.

The difference between these latter urban spaces and that of Italy resides in the purpose of their visitors. However, in order to discover an explanation, as well as the results of these activities, on the aforementioned spaces, the TALC may be applied in both cases.

When referring to the motivation of a tourists' visit to the Italian city of Venice, it is understood that their focus is on the historical-cultural aspects of the destination. In the case of the Costa del Sol, the visitor has the purpose in mind of a relaxing vacation, while enjoying the three S's, "sea," "sun," and "sand."

At the same time, the tremendous diversification and development of the tourism of Southern Spain should be highlighted. This phenomenon is accompanied, without a doubt, also, by misuse and overuse, which leads, just as in the case of Venice, to congestion in terms of the population, which spills on and contributes to the overcrowding of the infrastructures. This situation can be observed throughout the year but is especially manifested during the summer season.

There are more than 85 golf courses, which lie along the coast, from Cádiz to Málaga, as a sporting alternative to beach tourism. For those who find environmental tourism appealing, there is Lobo Park. As its name indicates, it is a highly acclaimed park, located in Antequera, dedicated to the conservation, and study of wolves, as well as animal behavior. The Picasso Museum in Málaga has been developed as a complementary cultural draw to the framework of these and the many more multiple tourist activities, which have appeared, especially, since the 80's of the 20th century in Spain.

All this leads to an overcrowding and strain on structures and resources, which experiences no relief, even though there has been a slight improvement with the construction of the N-340 highway. This so called "improvement" has nothing to do with safety, as this roadway boasts an average of 30 accidents per year, per kilometer, and is considered to be the most dangerous in Europe. (O'Reilly K. 2000).

On the other side of the spectrum, the construction of the AP-7 toll highway represents a tremendous display of engineering deployment and capabilities. However, this means of transportation is not usually enjoyed or preferred by the majority of the Andalusian people, due to the high costs of the toll for the driver. Therefore, the N-340 still maintains a needlessly high level of congestion, as once again, the force of economic determinism has intervened and physically directed the flow of traffic through the least expensive route, regardless of safety or efficiency.

Having said this, it can be deduced that in the Costa del Sol, as well as in other Mediterranean spaces, such as Venice, that tourism is certainly a very valuable industrial activity for the community. However, if uncontrolled, and left in an exaggerated manner, these locations lose their quality of life as centers of work and residence for their people.

In this way, tourism that is developed uncontrollably is not a viable approach for urban growth. In these cases, it is necessary to examine the development of the tourism market, in a limited space, and, at the same time, review the responses of the market supply. Also, the options and alternatives that the organizations and institutions, such as the Municipalities and Tourist Boards have at their disposal, in order to make tourism represent a benefit to society and not a detriment must be explored.

In the case of Venice, as has already been discussed, the destination is one of exclusively cultural tourism, which, when developed in a balanced way, means:

> "...an important resource for cities and regions. It provides solid opportunities for growth that are not limited to direct employment and revenue generation. A visitor-friendly environment enhances the quality of life of a place --- and consequently its capacity to attract new and strategic functions, contributing to general goals of urban development in the global economy."[132]

This statement, though intentionally referring to an urban tourist destination, may also be applied to a regional destination, such as the Costa del Sol, with a focus on its function as a space dedicated to tourism.

It can be sustained, as well as proven, in a study performed by Dzimbowska-Kowalska & Funck (2000), and which was cited by Russo, that in an environment where culture is present, in abundance, in the form of cultural heritage (historical buildings, and other such representations), as well as cultural activities, these sites serve to enrich and add prestige to the urban environment.

The cultural heritage, generally serves as a magnet, so to speak, to attract service enterprises, their employees and new residents, as well as tourists. In this way, tourism empowered by culture becomes the motivating force behind the regeneration of a city that, otherwise, would have fallen into tourist stagnation. In the case of the

---

[132] Antonio P. Russo et al., "Planning Consideration for Cultural Tourism: A Case Study of Four European Cities," *Tourism Management* 5, no. 23 (2002): 175

Costa del Sol, the vital force of its cities may also be the source of its economic regeneration.

Although, Russo maintains that making use of a city's cultural and historical resources may be a very attractive way of keeping with the social and economic development of the urban space. He cautions, however, that if this is not done with the balanced utilization of all its resources, the city may fall into a path of short-term sustainable economic development. As a result, the previously mentioned opportunities for cities, such as Venice and other European urban centers, to function as regional hubs for employment and residence, have been proven to disappear.

Because of this reason, the simple use of a city as a cultural attraction does not seem to be a solution for long-term balanced economic development. Conversely, upon extrapolating from urban to regional, it is necessary to formulate a balanced usage of resources, such as those belonging to the Spanish Costa del Sol. A clear example of this imbalance is the spatial overflow, which has occurred along this coastline, with the dense construction of golf courses, which has triggered the unbalanced consumption of the region's scarcity of the natural resource of fresh drinking water.

This dilemma of the best usage of the tourism resource, in the development of a city, more closely affects restricted urban centers, in which places such as Toledo, Spain can be included. Here the municipality encounters the difficulty of formulating a vital and healthy center at the socio-economical level. A management policy is needed that transcends beyond the simple flow of tourists to the city and, which has to do with traffic control, public health, as well as with the construction of appropriate infrastructure. By the same token, the small urban centers in the Costa del Sol also face this problem.

Even though the Western Hemisphere lacks the quantity of an urban tourist destination that Europe has, it cannot go unnoticed that the tourism journal published, in the West, *Annals of Tourism Research and Tourism Management* contains very few articles published on the subject of management of historical urban centers. This subject is found, and denominated, by Cazes and Potier in their book (1996), as a "scientific vacuum," and cited by Russo.

With the intention of satisfying this situation, in theory and practice, the TALC is examined and applied in the spatial sense, as opposed to what could be an application in the temporal sense. The intent is to accomplish this latter form of application, in the following chapter of this book. This location's reduced space is its most noteworthy characteristic and will be dealt with accordingly. The other characteristics of the urban center are presented, as a function of this restricted spatial variable.

THE VICIOUS CIRCLE MODEL AND THE TALC

In the first place, the case of Venice, along with the TALC theory could be assigned a theoretical model called the "vicious circle" (developed by Antonio Paolo Russo). This model describes how tourists select options for their stay in this location, based on their personal budget, which could negatively impact the income of the area, at the level of the Municipality.

This leads the tourists to seek lodging in the outskirts of the historical destination, as it is cheaper outside the urban center. The municipality loses income as a consequence of this dislocation. In the case of the Costa del Sol, this theory can be applied to the golf courses where the tourists find lodging in the resorts surrounding these installations, where water is consumed in tremendously abundant quantities.

Perhaps, the application of the TALC to a historical destination may cause it to lose some of its validity. In fact, it has been criticized by some scientists, when applying it to an urban context. Though, Russo contends that it still retains qualities of useful analysis. In the first place, Russo conceptualizes the development of the future and present relationships of the tourist industry with the economic, social or environmental sectors of a society at an evolutionary level. In this way, in many cases the spatial development of the historical destination takes place outside of the confines of the municipality and restriction exist with regard to this space.

Therefore, an analytical theory is necessary that bases itself on the TALC and is appropriate for it. Its application provides for a vision of the future, in a dynamic and complex municipality, where the focus is the development of tourism as a positive force. However, this is not always the case. In Venice, the number of tourism arrivals has triplicated in number, in recent years, and now, with this wave of visitors, danger is even forecasted for the welfare of the community.

This danger caused, by this influx of tourists, is also experienced in the Costa del Sol, where it is estimated that there have been indicators of saturation of this tourism element. For example, data from sources, such as different public and private enterprises, show the absolute saturation point figures going from 70,523 in Torremolinos in January of 1999 to 130,167 in December of that same year. In the same period of time, and in the same year, Marbella oscillated from 155,914 tourists to 260,860. (Navarro Jurado, E. 2003). Though these figures are not recent, it can be expected that these numbers have only continued to grow exponentially.

Here, it becomes necessary to take into consideration the definition and application of the carrying capacity theory, as is cited by Russo:

> "The number of visitors that an area can accommodate before negative impacts occur."[133]

However, this balance is the responsibility of the heads of the community. In the case of Venice, the number of resident tourists, as well as excursionists, who visit the city, continues to grow, but at the same time, the balance of the carrying capacity is surpassed. Russo reveals these definitions, and more to this effect, through Van den Berg, another expert, in the field, who writes:

> "*Real* excursionists are all those day-trippers who come to the visited city during the day from their normal place of residence and go back there in the

---

[133] B.S. Martin et al., "An Examination of the Relationship between Carrying Capacity and the Tourism Area Lifecycle: Management and Policy Implications." *Journal of Environmental Management* 31, no. 7 (1990): 329

evening: *Indirect* excursionists are all those who visit the city during the day coming from and going back to another place this the main destination of their journey..."[134]

Van den Berg ends with the following regarding his three-dimensional analysis of excursionists:

"*False* excursionists are all those day visitors that spend the night in a different place than the city itself that remains their main destination."[135]

However, the definition of the concept of carrying capacity and its negative impact, on the quality of the environment, given the excess number of tourists at a given time, and in a given space, is a subject that has not been completely clarified and is still debated, among those who study this subject. Conclusive findings still must be arrived at, as to whether upon reducing the number of visitors, the carrying capacity is surpassed because of the deterioration of the environment. At that point, it becomes a less desirable destination for visitors.

The possibility also exists that the carrying capacity is exceeded when "will to spend" has decreased, that is to say, when the tourist spends less in the destination. Normally, this situation occurs when the area becomes attractive to a segment of the population with less purchasing power. In other words, tourists either stop coming to the destination, or stop spending in the destination.

In the case of the Costa del Sol, the carrying capacity has been surpassed in both cases. It is surpassed, in the sense that the environment has deteriorated, which has led to a "decrease of the will to spend." The vicious cycle is apparent here, as tourists spend less, and the municipalities involved have decreased, in order to invest in infrastructures for the municipalities. This leads to an even greater deterioration of the environment and consequentially to a "lesser will to spend." In this manner, the multiple municipalities of the Costa del Sol are also protagonists in the process.

For Russo, when a city or any tourist destination experiences a decrease in foreign currency influx, the financial management and urban development will necessarily be involved in a series of multiple and negative impacts on the community. By defining the tourist destination's consequential cash inflow and outflow and, thus, underlining the quality of tourism that the area attracts, the TALC may be an aid in the discovery of what stage on the evolutionary cycle the destination is situated.

This information could determine if the destination is at the stage of "stagnation" or "pre-stagnation." If the average tourist spends less and the destination is mature, such as is the case with the Costa del Sol, this investigative study intends to prove, define and discover that said space is situated in the new evolutionary stage of the TALC, the "pre-stagnation" phase, which meets and explains the particular conditions of this coastline, and its municipalities.

---

[134] L. Van den Berg et al., "Urban Competitiveness, Marketing and the Need for Organizing Capacity," *Urban Studies* 36, (1999): 991.

[135] *Ibid.* pp. 991

According to Russo, a regionalization of the urban center of the tourism destination has already been established if the city receives less funds. That is to say, the visitors find lodging in the conglomerates of hotels located in the periphery of the urban center. In the Costa del Sol, these areas are located in spaces, which do not contribute to the municipality of the historic destination. In this way, the municipal expenditures, having to do with the tourism industry, such as general maintenance of infrastructures and the environment may only be achieved by a tax hike imposed on residents and industries, normally not related to this activity.

This economic burden for the residents, and the aforementioned industries, creates an environment in the urban center, which makes it unattractive as a place for the vital, as well as productive needs of these entities. The city becomes an unbalanced monoculture of tourism. To this end, Russo explains that the Venetian population has been reduced by more than 50 percent, in the last half of the past century.

In this way, the spatial analysis of the historical destination, when taken as a regional entity, explains the competence and behavior of both the private, as well as public activities of the central Municipality. The application of the TALC, in this case, may situate Venice, in the surprising state of stagnation, or the also applicable state of "pre-stagnation," devised for the first time in this study, and customized to the case of the Spanish Costa del Sol.

On the Spanish coast, the visitors seek their lodgings, in hotel in many cases, on the golf courses or they own houses, within the golf resorts, while consuming the scarce and, therefore, much desired water resources. The consumption of this resource is used mainly for the watering of their golf courses. These well and river resources become more expensive due to their scarcity. Consequentially, the cost of living, in general, rises for the resident population at large. Therefore, and in this way, much as in the case of Venice, this Spanish region also becomes a less feasible and attractive location for residence.

Russo transfers his focus from the TALC to the "vicious cycle theory," and his thoughts reflect the basic idea that when a tourist visits an historic destination, he or she does so with the purpose of experiencing the cultural attractions of the city or location. These, as well as the areas in which they are found, must be in good condition. The squares and museums must be cared for. The price, in the best possible situation, must be adjusted to the quality of the paintings and sculptures exhibited in these places.

Russo calls this center, in his previously mentioned article, the "HC," or the Historical Center. The first step, which defines the Historical Center and, which, at the same time, also represents its first problem, is that it overlaps what he has also defined and termed the Functional Tourist Region (FTR). This is the peripheral area where the tourists find lodging. It is a space outside the administrative limits of the tourist destination.

When applying the TALC theory, or the "vicious cycle" model, as an instrument at the level of spatial analysis, an estimation may be formulated, as to when the stage of stagnation or "pre-stagnation" has been reached. It may be concluded that a stage has been arrived at, where the hotel beds in the HC are not sufficient or not economically competitive. In this way, they cause an imbalance in favor of the Functional Tourism Region. In the case of Venice, the FTR may exceed its national border, incurring losses, even at the level of economy of the state, beyond the enclaves of its municipalities.

Given the fact that the Costa is a region, and not a municipality, it is dissimilar to an historical urban center such as Venice. However, many urbanized nuclei do exist, which are on the outskirts of the municipalities, simply because they are located around the extremely numerous golf courses, which are completely, isolated from the Andalusian culture. They offer services and welcome, in the best of all cases, the British, in the first place, and the Germans, in the second place.

The most glaring example is the La Cala Golf in Mijas. This is the largest golf complex, in all of Spain. Here, supposedly, only recycled water is used for the watering of the residents' sumptuous gardens, and crystal-clear swimming pools. In reality, a verbal conversation, with the Director, in situ, of said golf course, revealed that this space also uses drinking water, found in such scarcity, from a well, for these finalities.

Russo continues to suggest that, in a second application of the "vicious cycle" model to the evolution of a tourism area, visitors can be expected to cause considerable congestion for the center. The visiting pattern is less flexible, as it is found to depend on good weather and the festivities celebrated, in the space, pertaining to the center's exterior elements. Therefore, visitors become more seasonal. This happens in a major way in the Costa del Sol.

Also, visitors have, in general, less information, as to the content of the cultural products the urban center offers, which is the case of Venice and what the region offers, which is the case of the Costa del Sol. Tourists concentrate on fewer attractions, within the city, or in the golf courses, but in greater conglomerations. These elements have been termed "super-star attractions" (Towse R, 1991), when analyzing the economies of cities of art. To this end, it is found that visitors' extensive spending is greatly reduced.

This is exactly what occurs in the Costa del Sol. Tourists concentrate themselves in the beach municipalities or the golf course developments, eating their eggs with bacon and tomato, drinking beer, without enjoying the delicious gastronomy of that part of the Mediterranean. Also, in their great majority, such historical and cultural treasures of Andalucía, such as the "Pueblos Blancos," or "White Villages" go entirely unknown to the visitors. They also rarely, if ever, venture into the interior to become acquainted with the provincial capitals of Granada, Córdoba or Sevilla.

For Russo, what should be analyzed, in this third phase, is not the municipalities' loss of income, and its consequential increase in expenses, but the loss of the quality of the tourist experience. This inefficient, yet dynamic, organization allows the tourists to come from a spatially larger area, but they are also more ignorant as to the quality of the tourist experience. The service operators may take advantage of these less sophisticated, as well as less savvy consumers, and offer them a lesser quality tourist product. A higher echelon of tourists is lost in favor of groups, which tend to spend less.

These latter and less informed tourists are willing to sacrifice or ignore a product of better quality, in order to reduce their expenses. In this stage, an inexpensive level of the industry is superimposed on one of quality by standardizing it. What materializes, in this way, is what has been termed by various authors, as the "McDonaldization," of the sector. This means that at this stage, the esthetics of the cultural landscape of the city or of the region run the risk of becoming standardized. As this happens, these municipal spaces become littered with McDonald's and Burger King franchises appearing in their areas.

With regard to the fourth step of the "vicious cycle" model, Russo concludes with the same reasoning, with which he began, that is, its dynamics. In other words, the mechanics is derived from the fact that lodging in the center of the city, in terms of its price, and for that reason, did not adjust to the demand of that sector. This dynamic is found in the FTR, as central hotel beds are rejected in the HC.

The consequence of this situation is a combination of a lack of information, on one hand, and on the other the congestion caused by the tourists, as they concentrate in a small proportion of the cultural attractions. An imbalance arises, in this way, where certain tourism resources are supra-utilized, and others are ignored or underutilized. In general, a minority of visitors enjoy a lesser quantity of what the culture offers, in comparison with what the destination as a whole has to offer.

As a result, the attractions are less capable of generating capital gain. A large part of the tourist's budget is spent on souvenir type of expenditures or, at the same time, their funds are poorly administrated and squandered on lodging outside of the urban center and, therefore, do not benefit it in the least. In the case of the Costa del Sol, tourism along the Western coast, the beaches and golf courses, are over utilized and, therefore, there is very little transition from one municipality to the next.

Russo believes that this situation is observed, especially in the present, due to the fact that the central governments do not subsidize, or subsidize to a much lesser degree, these historical centers. The policy is one of "the user foots the bill." Therefore, it can be said that the expenditures of the visitors are used for the corresponding improvements and developments. This may be a workable situation if the peripheries where the tourists are lodged, fall within a taxation jurisdiction, which may be channeled and dedicated to the maintenance and enrichment of the cultural assets of the center. However, this, in many cases, does not occur.

In the Costa del Sol, a palpable phenomenon is observed, in which, it is the private enterprises that exploit the golf courses. It is done through what each golf player pays or what each owner contributes, through his or her home-owner costs as part of the development, where their residence is located. In reality, this is a less efficient policy, and a more expensive one, than would be the case of a golf course exploited by a municipal entity or the county. The latter occurs in Southern California, as exemplified by an analogous Mediterranean climate. In this location, the green fee prices to the public are much less than those of the Costa del Sol. The courses are in just as good conditions, as those on this Spanish coastline.

This cannot happen, as Russo previously stated, when the periphery takes free advantage of the center without contributing to its costs. It will also not occur, if the center is under pressure to grow and expand, which it will be unable to do, if in competition with the periphery, as the latter presents itself in a more desirable economic light. In this way, income that the center would normally receive, is lost and is, thus, channeled towards the periphery. This phenomenon may be extended to a region, where the HC exists in the same nation or it may include extra-national borders, where the country involved has absolutely no control.

The golf courses may be considered to be the RFT of the Costa del Sol. These, however, do fall within the autonomy of its national borders, though, in many cases they represent foreign fiefdoms, within the scenario of national tourism. Just one example of these cases is the previously mentioned La Cala Golf de Mijas, which is exploited by a group of Irish investors.

This application of the "vicious cycle" model can explain the stagnation of a tourist destination, as the TALC also explains it. Scientists cited by Russo such as (Tremblay 1998) and that by (Keane 1997) study the subject as well. They both underline how the fragmented and preindustrial nature of tourism did not allow for the fall in the quality of the destination's supply and demand to be foreseen until this phase of the cycle had already been established. Here, the tourist peripheral region, or the FTR, or the CH, may be cited and defined as "strategic spaces," as they may be definitive for the life of the tourism destination given the spending incurred and the time spent in both spaces.

Russo says that markets may not differ one from the other, but this does not happen with cities. To begin with, the quality of life worsens for the residents when an impacting relationship between visitors and tourists exists. With this pressure, the space may become uninhabitable and contentious. The first group may need to leave the downtown space, in order to find shopping centers, with more affordable prices. This may lead to access problems, as well as overcrowding in the public areas. Russo approaches this subject, by going back to a classical theory, but still very applicable (Tiebout 1956) to the existing situation. This specialist says that residents may even have to move out of their homes, in order to adjust their income to the market value of the city's real estate.

According to Van den Berg, when this option is not available:

> "…if a tourist city wishes to diversify its economy and become less dependent on a highly unstable industry like tourism, it needs to project an image of an attractive and convenient location that sells value for money."[136]

This occurs in the downtown centers of the Costa del Sol, especially, during the summer seasons, when the overcrowding of people and traffic, in municipalities such as Torremolinos, may become unbearable. It can be said, without a doubt, that he who does not live well from tourism—lives badly.

---

[136] *Ibid.* pp.994.

ALTERNATIVES TO STAGNATION

According to Russo, the establishment of the "vicious cycle" can be avoided, in a historical center and in any tourism destination, if a few steps are followed.

In the first place, the number of hotel beds should be increased in the downtown area, in order to decrease the tendency of regionalization. If this is an impossible feat to accomplish, then an intent should be made, with the of object of better planning, in order to reduce urban congestion, by improving connections between the downtown center and the periphery, aside from other urban centers in the Costa del Sol.

At the same time, a more compact tourist destination should be designed. Also, a policy of maximization of computer resources should be implemented, in order to better inform the tourist about the availability of alternative attractions, which the destination offers. This policy should be put into practice, in order to avoid unplanned or spontaneous excursions.

Finally, Russo believes that there is a tendency to omit the cultural destinations' budget. This happens with more preponderance in the last phase of the cycle. The tax revenues are distributed in a widely spread array of municipal objectives. If the income, which generates the cultural assets and tourism attractions, were to be destined for the exclusive improvement and enrichment of these attractions, by means of an appropriate cultural policy, the HC, or the urban center, would maintain their level of quality. This could even continue if they were to face a downfall in the tourist market. Perhaps, the quantity of the quality of tourists who seek lodging in the urban center might also increase.

In the case of the Costa del Sol, in order to avoid the "vicious cycle," it is necessary to seek out a methodology of spatial management, in order to reduce the intra-urban, as well as the interurban congestion. It is not necessary to build towering hotel structures, which are only an eyesore to the stunning Costa del Sol shoreline. More publicity campaigns could be created, regarding the historical attractions of the region, thereby lessening the density of tourists along the seashore.

Municipal income should be used for a maximization of resources at the level of health and the adequate supply of drinking water. All this should be accomplished, with the goal of attracting a better quality of tourists and improving residents' lives. As Russo states, a well-developed tourist industry is, also, the basis for healthy municipal economic development, at every level.

However, and in spite of all the aforementioned strategies, in Venice, it is necessary to recognize that cultural tourism is an asset in and of itself. It has no utility that goes beyond its own identity. It is not like sea, sun and sand or golf, for that matter, which all contain the objective of entertainment. That is why it is more difficult to maintain and develop tourism in an historical destination. In this case, and for this reason it is necessary to protect it with additional measures of support that go beyond the traditional ones.

In the first place, the cultural supplies, which are already present in the destination, could be amplified and diversified. For example, concerts could be fomented, or plays could be presented in the parks and squares of the downtown center. This would be an articulation of the concept of rejuvenation. In the second place more services could be added, such as cafeterias, libraries, or electronic files to such places as museums. Another possibility would be to increase the artistic supply through the augmentation of art galleries.

In exchange for all these resources, a market value price would be charged. To this end, the visitors' awareness of the intrinsic value of the place's cultural supply would increase. Therefore, it is expected that as the tourist increases his or her appreciation of historic assets, so will increase his or her disposition to pay for them.

Also, some light, as well as hope, could be shed on the peripheral tourist region, which has been considered to be such an unproductive, as well as problematic entity for the center. It could contain a series of poles, where tourism attractions are inserted, converting it into an opportunity for sustainable development, instead of a burden for the HC.

For the enrichment of Venice, and according to Russo, all this, of course, must be accomplished through the strengthening and direction of the systematic nature of the cultural sector. That is to say, this sector is based exclusively on the cultural wellbeing of the tourists' space. It depends on a necessary, coordinated marketing strategy, as well as one of communication, which will increase the supply of cultural products to a market of demand. This goal should be accomplished by means of a strong direction focused on the sources of the tourism markets.

In the Costa del Sol and in the Costa del Golf, nicknamed as such, for those who seek their form of entertainment in the practice of this sport, a marketing campaign can be formulated, if the previous steps are followed. This should be done, and in fact, is taking place, with the purpose of attracting more affluent tourism, with more purchasing power.

Currently, and according to verbal interviews, at the Río Real Monteros de Marbella and Golf La Cala de Mijas, these campaigns are directed mainly towards Great Britain. The British are aware that their strong sterling pound currency goes a long way, in terms of purchasing power, along this Spanish coastline. These publicity campaigns could be increased, and expanded to include other countries, while simultaneously targeting tourists with a greater spending capacity.

THE PARADOX OF THE TOURISM INDUSTRY

Although, these steps mentioned by Russo do not appear to mention anything new, in terms of the development of tourist destination, sadly, their application, in reality, is the exception to the rule. In the past, the policy of historical municipalities and also those of the Costa del Golf, has been to separate the tourism development from the basic economy of the city, and that of the region. This occurred to keep the region from utilizing the city as its structural motivating force.

Also, a distinction has not been made between the excursionist demand, and that of the tourists, or those that simply come to hide away in the housing developments, located in the circumferences of the golf courses. This spatial reality has caused an imbalance between the sector's true and false income and expenditures. Therefore, there are existing areas in Europe, in general, and in the Costa del Sol, in particular, which are unable to enjoy a sustainable usage of their spaces.

Venice, by comparison is a super star, in this sense, as it, perhaps, enjoys the reputation of being the most famous tourist destination in the world. The Costa del Sol may also be considered a super star, upon arriving at the stage of saturation. However, the saturation is not regarding hotel beds, but instead, with regards to the usage of its scarce resource, water, as well as sanitation maintenance.

According to Russo, the Venetian tourist industry is a paradox. On one hand, it is the only economic sector in the HC that continues to thrive. On the other, the industry is considered to be the culprit, in causing such decay in the city. It generates many management problems and municipal maintenance costs. Its HC is in the heart of the lagoon where Venice is located. It is a problematic space, as it is periodically flooded. However, its principal area is found in an economic region, which is fully developing.

In the Costa del Sol, the industry is also a paradox. Tourism generates the most income for the region, yet it is also the activity, which most saps its sacred water supply. Also, this prosperity is undervalued by infrastructure problems, which create a level of sanitation, traffic, parking, public transportation and deterioration of the environment in general.

According to Russo, the proportion of visitors and residents reached 50 to 1, in the year 2000. It even arrived at 175 to 1, if the excursionists are included. These tourists come to see the city, in its entirety, as it offers the greatest display of architecture of the past 13 centuries, invaluable art collections and top quality cultural events. It is believed that the entire city should be considered as a piece of art given its urban fabric, atmosphere, channeling of waters and constructed space. In fact, UNESCO has already given it this designation.

In the Costa del Sol, between 2005 and 2010, it is estimated that there will be a constructed space, which perhaps doses not qualify as a historical center (HC), containing as great a concentration of art. However, this destination does offer the visitor entertainment, in the form of sea, sun and sand. Additionally, there is golf, as well as a sports complex in Benalmádena, along with the delicious local gastronomy, as well as interesting culture, which provide quite the variety of activities for the tourists.

Russo cites the figures (Canestrelli and Costa 1991), of 22,500 visitors per day, as the carrying capacity, but only a maximum of these individuals are excursionists. These are the figures, which are set, in order to maintain the full functionality of Venice's subsystems, used both by its residents and tourists. These elements include public transportation, garbage collection, as well as access to cultural assets. That is to say, these represent the socioeconomical carrying capacity of the urban system. According to these authors, in 1987, this limit was surpassed during 156 days, and since then, these transgressions have only continued to increase.

The RTF, which was mentioned earlier, plays a very important role in the spatial distribution of Venice, given the fact that it is enormous. This city represents a case where the region, in which it is located, extends further beyond its own jurisdiction, into countries such as Austria or Slovenia. Also, an "indirect tourism" is generated in the direction of Venice, coming from the nearby coastal region, which adds to the general influx of visitors.

Even though, no recent figures are available, at this time, it can be estimated that 80% of the visitors arriving in Venice are excursionists and that they spend more than 60% of their budget in lodging outside the HC. Their behavior proves the modality of the characteristics of the "vicious cycle," as this group generates more expenditures for the municipality than revenue.

In the Costa del Sol, the majority of visitors that generate revenue are British, followed by Germans. There is an unequal distribution of Scandinavian, tourists from the Netherlands and France. In this Spanish destination, the tourists settle in the RTF. They separate into groups of their own countries of origin. This is why a distinction must be made between the Venetian region and the region of the Costa del Sol.

The International Center for Economical Arts (ICEA), in 1997, performed a survey, which summarized the following information regarding the spatial behavior of visitors, according to these main directives. It was proven that 66 percent of the daily influx of people and vehicles, is found to be concentrated, within a few hours, during the morning, and once again, during that same time span, in the afternoon. The average stay in Venice was calculated at eight hours, but three-fifths of all visits were found to be shorter than this. It was also discovered that the accumulation of the flow of arrivals reach the city by means of their only connection, being the roadways or railways, with the main mass of the city. This causes great congestion on the main routes between this terminal and its other poles.

In the Costa del Sol, as has already been discussed, the main transportation artery is the N-340, which proves to be an insufficient means of movement during the summer seasons. The toll AP-7 freeway, though modern and a product of a much more advanced technology, is too expensive for continued use by a driver with an average income. The latter does not resolve the problem of extended and generalized traffic congestion.

Therefore, with so little time and information available to the visitor, the tourist stays are a function of the time and space available to the visitor. Their visits are motivated by the location of the downtown center or the golf course, which is the closest to their lodgings, and the route they take to travel there. This pattern of behavior, on the part of the tourist is supported by Towse's theory, which identifies Venice as a superstar. Also, the individual attraction of the downtown centers may be considered superstars, in a larger urban universe, given the concentration of visitors, which some attract, according to their distribution in the cultural space.

For Russo, given the congestion, the spatial location of the attractions and the lack of information, at the tourists' disposal, some of the cultural assets are infra-utilized and others supra-utilized by the tourist population. Altogether, many visitors may see and explore fewer cultural attractions than the HC has to offer. Data, even exists, that suggests that only one in every 4.4 visitors purchases a ticket for a museum, and only one in 55.7 visitors enters a church if a price for admission is charged.

TOURISM GROWTH AND VICIOUS CYCLE MODEL SPATIAL CONSIDERATIONS

Russo continues to apply his "vicious cycle" model to the degree that cultural assets are not the only elements which are not consumed at the desirable level for economic sustainability. Unfortunately, the majority of information to be had is with reference to lodging. Regarding this economic sector, it also seems to be affected by the "vicious cycle."

Within Venice's downtown center, there are two main types of hotels. There are those that were built around San Marcos square, at the beginning of the 20th Century, which are the most expensive. Their rates are based on their prestige. Then, there are those hotels that are located, in the area of the pathways, which lead from the central station to the square. These are newer, but also expensive. Their rates are based on their accessibility to the points of interest of the city.

In the Costa del Sol, lodging is polarized around popular centers, such as Torremolinos, or the more expensive nuclei, which include Marbella and Sotomayor. The more than 86 golf courses which currently exist allow for revenue at the level of lodging for house, apartment and hotel room rentals, at a great variety of prices along the western coast.

The most successful auxiliary industries, such as souvenir shops, nightclubs, as well as street vendors are also located in the most central areas of the CH. Following the model of the "vicious cycle," these enjoy the demand of the least and most poorly informed tourism sector. There also, in the case of the Costa del Sol, the most successful businesses are located in the downtown centers.

Russo states that this model has two effects. On one hand, the traditional result is found, where tourism activity overcomes and takes over residential activity. However, what is emerging, in the present, is the situation where high-quality tourism is being supplanted by one of low quality. Even in high demand seasons, the rooms in high quality hotels remain vacant. This is occurring ever more frequently. A similar situation is taking place in the Costa del Sol. For this reason, and in this destination, every effort is made to implement purposeful tourism policies, which have the finality to attract a lesser quantity, but a greater quality of visitors.

Also, the number of repeat visitors to Venice is in decline. Even though, it has been suggested (Darnell & Johnson 2001) that there is a loss of interest in a tourist destination of visitors with high purchasing power, this does not necessarily mean that the destination has fallen into the stagnation stage. Although, it is significant to note that those in a position of less purchasing power, belonging to the consumer sector, obviously are less solvent and therefore represent less sustainable behavior in that sense.

An expansion of markets of new origin does not necessarily symbolize a healing or an improvement of the tourism market. However, in order to avoid stagnation in the Costa del Sol, this mature tourism destination prefers "to take no prisoners" and continues to seek out a higher caliber of tourists with greater purchasing power.

One of these new markets could be group tourism, as opposed to that of the individual type. At present, it is estimated that group visitors make up 32 percent of the total tourism activity. These tour operators are in the process of selling tours to locations, which are more and more distant from the Venetian HC.

Interviews have been conducted, with selected tour operators, who confirm that there is a direct relationship between the cost of the vacation package, and the distance it is located from the downtown center. Even though, no precise information is available, currently to this effect, it may be affirmed that tour operators are selling, with more frequency, vacation packages, which include stays at the golf courses, in the Costa del Sol. These holidays can be obtained at a great variety of prices.

On the contrary, and in Venice, the following phenomenon occurs:

> "...repeat visitors are the most likely to spend the night in the hinterland of Venice: those who have already visited the city, their return are likely to come as 'false excursionists'."[137]

To this end, Russo concludes that the preponderance of excursions as a means to visit the city of Venice, supposes a lessening of the possibility of saturation of the centrally located hotel rooms. At the same time, it is the result of a decision to consider the perceived costs of spending the night within the city of Venice.

Consequentially, the "vicious cycle" model proves that the distorted elements of the city's tourism usage feed off of themselves, creating even greater distortion. The city is visited, with a lack of information and with a consideration for costs, expressing, therefore, an appreciation, only for the most centrally located tourism spaces. These attractions, because of an excess in demand, become growingly more expensive.

On a second level, the centrally located hotels also become increasingly more expensive, because they must cover their costs of maintenance, as they find themselves to a great degree vacant. The tourist population has found lodging in the TFR, where the hotel rooms are less expensive. Therefore, the city's cultural assets generate, ever decreasing revenue. The centrally located, increasingly more expensive hotel rooms cause, in this way, an effect of rejection to any possible demand. Lastly, only the central auxiliary industries profit, though they damage the tourist industry of Venice, in general, by lowering its quality.

The model of the "vicious cycle" does not occur in the same way on the Costa del Sol. However, in applying it to a historical center (HC), such as Venice, it has to do with the infra-utilization or supra-utilization of the tourism product. That is to say, it deals specifically with the infra-utilization of the downtown center, if the functional regional center or FTC, is over utilized. This leads to the imbalance of certain tourist attractions in the historical center, or HC. It is understood that some are visited more than others.

Another consideration, in the Costa del Sol, is that the application of the "vicious cycle" model has to do with the unbalanced consumption of water. The more golf courses, which are developed, along this coast, that do not use recycled water for their irrigation, the less sustainable the development of the tourist industry becomes.

---

[137] P. Costa et al., "Venice and its Visitors: A Survey and a Model of Qualitative Choice." *Journal of Travel and Tourism Marketing* 4, no. 3 (1995): 67.

How then, can the "vicious cycle" model be related to the TALC? According to Russo, the TALC is not a valid method to forecast decline. That is to say, a tourist destination may already be in that stage, before the TALC recognizes it as such. The "vicious cycle" has an economic quality, and therefore contains a quantitative approach. This numerical nature allows municipal administrators, tourist board council members and government officials to formulate policies based on information regarding the "willingness to spend" of the average tourist, along with the scarcity of cubic meters of water.

Also, a quantitative survey could be done on residents' dissatisfaction, due to lack of water, as well as the pressure of the taxation policies experienced in certain urban nuclei, along the coast. With the application of the "vicious cycle," a study could also be made of the emigration of residents to other regions, as occurred in Venice, due to the contentious character of the place.

In the final analysis, both the TALC theory, as well as that of the "Vicious Cycle," may be used to define and explain a tourism destination's situation. The "Vicious Cycle" analyzes it and the TALC defines it within a specific theoretic framework.

FINAL CONSIDERATIONS

The "vicious cycle" theory is used by Russo, in the analysis of the spatial dimension, upon applying it to Venice's (CH) and its functional tourist region (FTR). This scientist applies the premise of a balanced tourism policy being beneficial for a city, such as the case of Venice, or a region, such as the case of the Costa del Sol. He sustains that, in this way, an ample gamma of tourist activities may create an economic recuperation.

However, in order for this equilibrium to take place in the urban center, as well as in the region, there needs to be a form of management, which goes beyond the formulation of infrastructures. A policy directed towards tourist and traffic control, as well as a valid improvement of the condition of public health, is needed. True scientific planning of the urban space, in the case of Venice, and of the regional space, in the case of the Costa del Sol is necessary.

Venice is struggling with the parasitism, of the already discussed functional tourism region (FTR), which feeds on the cultural attractions of the downtown hub of urban Venice, but which does not contribute, proportionately, to the economic life of the city. It also creates congestion on the roadways and railways, between the hub, and the functional center.

The Costa del Sol is experiencing a similar situation, in that it is a region composed of small urban spaces, as well as an excessive number of golf courses, which are drastically depleting its drinking water resources. In this way, it is becoming an area, dangerously, lacking in this basic necessity for survival. Water is becoming expensive, but most importantly, it is becoming scarce. Scarce, to the point, of converting this coastal space into a conflictive and uninhabitable place, in which to reside or to work.

In both cases, there is an existing policy of noninterventionism, on behalf of the municipal and provincial authorities. A philosophy has been imposed, in which, it is the consumer who pays, and the private entities that administer the institutions. This scenario is, especially, found in the Costa del Sol, with regard to the golf courses, where it is the foreigners who manage and administrate these installations.

With this strategy, the tourist seeks to lower his or her expenses, and in many cases, sacrificing the quality of a more sophisticated tourism experience. Therefore, in Venice, visitors find lodging in the periphery of the region and in the Costa del Sol the sports aficionados stay at the golf courses, surrounded by standardized and artificial landscaping, without participating in the Andalusian culture.

All these characteristics represent the passage from the stage of mature tourism to one of stagnation, analyzed by the spatial theory of the "Vicious Cycle" and defined in the specific framework of the theory of the "Tourism Area Life Cycle." If Russo's spatial theory is applied first, it may be possible to remedy the economic and natural resource problems that these destinations are experiencing. They can avoid falling into the stage of "pre-stagnation," devised by this study, or stagnation, upon reaching the maximum carrying capacity. At that point, the tourist may have lost his or her "will to spend" because of the economic, environmental or social deterioration of the place.

CHAPTER 6

The TALC, in Relation to the Costa Del Sol, in its Temporal Perspective

In the same manner in which Russo applied the Tourism Area Life Cycle theory (TALC) to the urban area of Venice, along with his own theoretical concept of the "vicious cycle," the validity of the TALC may also be submitted for study in the temporal dimension. This was first accomplished by Sandra Corak, upon identifying historical stages, on the Croatian coast, thus identifying it as a tourist destination.

Corak states, this sense:

> "In this study, the life cycle model is used to determine the stages and analyze the Opatija Riviera, a destination that has been developing tourism for more than 150 years. The TALC is applied to identify four distinct stages, and it is argued that those stages could, also be analyzed as separate life cycles."[138]

This researcher states, at the same time, the additional value she views in the TALC concept, with its strategic options could help destination managers and planners to "reinvent," this heritage resort on the Adriatic Coast.

---

[138] Sandra Corak, "The Modification of the Tourism Area Life Cycle Model for (Re)inventing a Destination: The Case of the Opatija Riviera, Croatia," in *The Tourism Area Life Cycle Vol. 1: Applications and Modifications,* R.W. Butler ed., (Clevedon: Channel View Publications, 2006), 271.

The Stages of the Tourism Life Cycle Theory Applied Temporally to the Costa del Sol, Spain							
Stage	Period I Before 1865	Period II 1865-1914	Period III 1919-1936	Period IV 1936-1939	Period V 1939-1950	Period VI 1950-1976	Period VII 1976-Until the Present
Exploration	Partially	Completety	Completely	Parttally	Completely	Completely	Completely
Participation	No	Partially	Partially	Partially	Completely	Completely	Completely
Development	No	No	Partially	No	Partially	Completely	Completely
Consolidation	No	No	No	No	No	Completely	Completaly
Pre-Stagnation	No	No	No	No	No	Partially	Completely
Stagnation	No	No	No	No	No	No	Partially
Rejuvenation	No	No	No	No	No	No	?
Source: Author's own elaboration based on Butler, Richard (1972).							

This chapter has the intention of formulating the different historical stages of tourism development in the Costa del Sol. Then, the different phases of the TALC will be applied to these phases, in order to determine which have been completed and at what temporal point this has occurred. That is to say, the evolutionary structure of phases of the development of the TALC will be applied to the historical stages of tourism periods of the Costa del Sol.

It is important to note the pertinence of organizing these stages in chronological order. The interpretation of the TALC, regarding the evolution of the case of the Costa del Sol, is schematized in the following chart. Later on, the region's historical development is discussed.

In this study, the different periods of historical development of tourism in the Costa del Sol are formulated. Next, the different phases of the TALC will be applied to these stages, in order to prove, which have been completed, and in what temporal moment this has taken place. In the final analysis, this chapter targets, as well as defines, the application of the evolutionary structure of the developmental phases of the TALC to the historical stages of the tourism periods in the Costa del Sol.

THE ORIGINS OF TOURISM DEVELOPMENT IN THE COSTA DEL SOL: THE EXPLORATION STAGE

In order to begin this socio-historical study, it is first necessary to define the means of transportation travelers to the Costa del Sol use in the greatest number. It can be said that the first responsible mechanism, which brought foreigners into this area in considerable numbers, was the construction of the railway, which arrived from Córdoba to Málaga in approximately 1865. The arrival of tourists began to surge, with the inauguration of the first railroad. However, this stage might have been more productive, if it had been accompanied by a greater and more stable exploitation of iron. The following has been written about this event: "The arrival of the railroad brought ruin to these mule-drawn diligences, which was followed by the abandonment of riding paths, which, gradually, became ill kept." [139]

The same authors have the following quote, containing a panoramic description, of these changing times, in terms of space and population, which this invention, or product, of the industrial revolution caused:

"...the railroad is responsible for the revolution in communications, which evolved a hundred years later. It opened the rich, and apparently seamless vein, which would make the Costa del Sol one of the preferred tourist destinations. The railways, considerably cheapened, the trips, shortened travel time, and increased the comfort vested in these junkets [140]

These authors continue:

"Then came the paved roads, the highways, and charter flights. Now streets, villages and beaches are strewn with crowds of foreigners moving, in every direction. The landscape has changed, and the form of life has changed."

Also, in terms of transportation infrastructure, Andalucía joined—with other possible sources of providers, explorers, or visitors—through a network of steam ships. These methods of travel, be they by land or sea, can be summarized in the following paragraph:

"Regular steamer services ran from London, often on a weekly basis, Liverpool also weekly and South Hampton fortnightly. These journeys took about a week to reach Gibraltar, Cádiz, Córdoba and Málaga. The fortnightly service from New York to Gibraltar took about eight or nine days. There were also regular services from Marseilles, Hamburg and Bremen."

They continue their thoughts on this matter, by writing:

"A major barrier to this mode of transport was, however the custom house formalities, in Spanish ports, where 'inadequate arrangements' and delays were common. The recommended method of travel to Spain was, therefore by rail via Paris (Lavaur, 1976). Paris to Madrid took about 32 hours but once in Spain, the railway system was considered generally 'unsatisfactory'."

---

[139] Andrés Arenas Gómez et al., Viajeros y turistas en la Costa del Sol: De Rilke a Brenan (Málaga: Miramar, 2003), 21.
[140] *Ibid.* pp. 21

Their description continues:

> "Express trains, rarely, ran faster than 25 m.p.h. and ordinary trains achieved less than 15 m.p.h. Anything but first class was to be avoided. By the end of the nineteenth century, mule-drawn diligences were rarely used except in parts of Andalucía."

However, before analyzing the ways and means of the arrival of these excursionists to the region, it is necessary, in order to have a better comprehension of the purpose of this study, to distinguish between the tourist and the traveler. The traveler ventures on foot, on horseback or by mule-drawn diligences. This form of travel led to a more intimate contact with the vegetation, climate and people, as well as the customs of place. In many cases, the traveler did not even have a predisposition in mind of what the purpose of his trip would be or what it would entail in the Andalusian space.

This is the case of the writer Gerald Brenan, who came to seek refuge in Málaga, after fighting in World War I. He became so enticed by the city, that after visiting it for the first time, he returned to its location to establish there his permanent home. His life in Málaga, became the inspiration for the movie entitled South of Granda (Colmo 2003). It reflects scenes of his life in the Alpujarras, as well as those which reflected his relationship with the mother of his only daughter.

Laurie Lee may also be placed in the category of a traveler. He traveled from one point to the next, on foot and playing a violin, in order to eke out a meager living. This is how he is described by Arenas and Majada: "young Lee appeared in the area of Málaga, in mid-autumn, around the middle of the 30's, on his way from Gibraltar. He unhurriedly walked along the coastal road, enjoying his surroundings."

Lee is quoted as having said:

> "It took me five days, following a zigzag road between the mountain and the sea, five days opening a path through the dazzling light, between growths of warm algae, thyme and mollusks."

Another traveler who became a permanent resident of the region, was Sir Peter Chalmers-Mitchell, or as he was affectionately called with the Andalusian phonetics, "Sopita." In 1932, he turned 68 and decided to retire in Málaga, where he already owned a house and, seasonally, would spend long periods of time there. He authored a book entitled My House in Malaga, in which he spoke of the "dolce vita" enjoyed by the British residents of that city.

Although Sir Peter's intentions were to live out the last days of his life in Málaga, he eventually had to flee the region, leaving his lifestyle and house behind at the start of the Spanish Civil War. He left on an American battleship headed for England. There, in his homeland, he was tragically run over by a bus, losing his life, never being able to accomplish his final wish of viewing his last sunset in Málaga.

The role women travelers played as travelers to the Costa del Sol is not less noteworthy than their male counterparts. Therefore, it is possible to mention the already well-known author, Rose Macaulay, as she adventured through the region.

She dedicated a book to a solo automotive trip she made in the 40's, along the Mediterranean Coast from Portbou to Gibraltar.

Macaulay made the same journey that a Greek navigator had made 2,500 years earlier. This trip led to the first written travel guide regarding "malakat," the name the Phoenicians baptized the city of Málaga with, meaning "place of passing." The difference between these two journeyers is that she made the trip, by land, and in the opposite direction, that is, from northeast to northwest.

Another important representative of the female gender role, in the Costa del Sol, is Penelope Chetwode, who preferred a less mechanized mode of transportation. This lady, around 1961, rode around the Andalusian mountains on the back of her most loyal and loved companion "Marquesa." This lovely mare shares the main character role, in the novel written by this English traveler and author entitled, Two Middle-Aged Ladies in Andalucía.

As is apparent, the English nationality predominates, in the case, of all the previously mentioned travelers. This is because the history of explorers of other European nationalities, such as the French, German, and to a lesser degree, the Danes, Dutch and Swedes, still remains to be revealed. Even though figures are not available, in this respect, what is well defined is the temporal period in which these visits took place.

Upon analyzing the historicism of the traveler, it is necessary to make a comparison with the tourist. As was previously discussed, the traveler begins an activity, spontaneously, and motivated by vital and personal necessities. The tourist, on the other hand, plans his trip to the very last minute and detail. His or her trip is motivated by a social necessity, or by the need to "keep up with the Joneses."

A particular vacation may represent a status symbol, such as a trip to Europe for Americans, or vice versa. The traveler has no knowledge of what awaits him, or her, at the turn of every corner. It is an experience, which is impossible, as well as diametrically opposed to being covered by a travel insurance policy that provides protection for the tourist. Whereas the traveler moves in small groups of people, with whom he is already familiar, the tourist sightsees collectively.

Perhaps, the most noteworthy comparison is what was discussed earlier, the traveler, in his or her adventure, develops a more intimate relationship with the flora and fauna of the place, as well with its cultural society. The tourist, on the other hand, only enjoys the micro-culture of his minutiously planned experience. In the Costa del Sol, that usually represents the three S's of "sea, sun and sand," as well as golf. Having established these differences between tourist and traveler, their temporal presence, in the Costa del Sol—and also in Spain in general—as each is seeking a different experience.

Since the 16th century, the elite tourism, and here, travelers deserve more consideration, as they centered their attention on France and Italy. Even though, to the south of Rome terrible lodging and road conditions persisted, as well as threats from bandits, travelers would, inevitably, select this region over Spain. The Spanish cultural element was not attractive enough, compared to that of France or Italy, to even begin to overcome these obstacles. Going back as far as to the empire of Phillip III, Northern European Protestants feared visiting Spain because of the inquisition.

There was also the belief that the court of this monarchy was far too serious, dark, as well as austere, compared to the Parisian "joie de vivre," or the already decadent Venice. This unfavorable image that the rest of Europe had, regarding Spain, began early on and continued well into the 18th Century. During this time, it was even considered to be as uncivilized as an African country.

In Iberian history, since Carthage to Ancient Rome, the idea of the periphery, continued to be perpetuated. Also, due to the Muslim invasion and the 700-year settlement which followed, an aura of "orientalism" was created, which was projected externally from a major part of the peninsula. Only a small parade of British subjects, from the enclave of Gibraltar, had the courage to penetrate, and explore the Southern coast of the Mediterranean. This, mainly, began to take place during the Romantic Period, however, insignificant numbers had also made previous incursions.

A decree in 1571, which prohibited the entrance of British subjects into the Spanish kingdom and also required special permits for the entrance of other foreigners was a discouraging obstacle for any traveler who wished to make the effort to visit the peninsula. Though, as Mead writes, there were some cautious tourists who still had the desire to visit what was considered to be a very exotic space:

> "The few who did, however, extended the cautious seventeenth century travel pattern into a distinct seasonal tour of the cultural centers of the peninsula, which was to endure for the next two hundred years."

And Mead continues:

> "Based on the autumn and winter season, a handful of tourists explored Burgos, Valladolid, Segovia, and Madrid, followed by Toledo, Córdoba, Sevilla, Cádiz, Gibraltar, Málaga, Cartagena, Murcia, Alicante, Valencia and Barcelona. Other itineraries included Zaragoza, Aranjuez, Salamanca, and León."

All these negative attitudes changed, however, with the advent of Romanticism. What had been seen as negative characteristics of Spanish society in the 16th and 17th centuries became an opposite pole of attraction, as the romantic spirit sought out the exotic. This could be found in the customs of medieval Spain, its Moorish heritage and picturesque folklore, as well as, up until that time, its indomitable landscapes. Spain went to being, in the same sphere of interest, as Egypt, and Greece occupied, instead of occupying the lesser magnetic rung of such unappealing countries, as Russia, Poland, or Scandinavia, in previous centuries.

Yet, it was not the high class that attracted this new wave of visitors to Spain and removed it from the cultural European periphery. The popular culture—with its bullfights, typical festivities and costumes, among other things—was what served as a magnet to draw these foreign visitors into its cradle. Also, it was usually the Andalusian culture, which served as the typical Spanish tourist symbol.

To this end, it was not unusual to find other regions and provinces that began in order to imitate Andalucía's tourist-draw, the construction of bullfighting rings and caves for gypsies, even though these elements were not genuine elements of their culture. Aside from its exotic culture, as well as landscape, Spain also began to represent a cheaper and less developed travel destination.

The romantic travelers were more attracted to this option than, for example, the French Riviera, as they found the former to be just as healthy as the latter. Therefore, it is revealed that an intent was made to develop Málaga as a winter tourism destination during the first half of the 19th century. Unfortunately, this development was only, moderately and irregularly, successful throughout this historical period. Reasons, such as these found in Baedecker's narration can explain the lack of development of this Mediterranean destination:

> "A vigorous effort has been made of recent years to 'boom' Málaga as a winter resort, but its success is severely hindered by the dirt of the streets and the inefficiency of the drainage system. The lack of dust-free promenades is also much felt while the comparative deficiency of really comfortable quarters and of the means of amusement and distraction cannot be left out of account.

It is already mentioned that, during that time period, Málaga lacks drinking water, for its growing population. This is a timeless, recurring, and still a present theme in the region. It is also precisely the motive for this study. For this reason, and in this conclusive research, that upon applying the stages of development of the TALC to the Costa del Sol, it is found to be in the stage of stagnation or "pre-stagnation," the phase discovered by the analysis of this book, precisely, for its application to this coastline, but also applicable to other tourist destinations. This is said because the scarce resource of water is not sufficiently available for its numerous needs of consumption.

However, it may be said that, historically, there was a thriving tourism of spas, in Málaga, as well as in Carratraca, which welcomed such renown personalities as Byron, Dumas and Doré, in spite of the negative image projected of the place, principally by the British. It is worth mentioning that there was a rest home, which was attended to by a British physician, perhaps, as a precursor of the possibilities of the place as a space for rest and relaxation.

It can be said, that during this period, Spain was a far cry from being one of the main European tourist attractions. Italy and France were the "super star" tourist attractions of Europe, mainly because the British gave Spain a very negative reputation. This was based on the religious and imperial rivalry, between the two countries, which had been established, since the 16th century. Richard Ford, one of the best British chroniclers of travel in Spain, who was known to exaggerate and decry the conditions presented in the country, made the following classification regarding Spanish inns: "…Spanish inns according to three categories—'bad, worse and atrocious' and advised prospective travelers to bring their own provisions."

Therefore, it may be ascertained that only the first stage of the TALC, that is the exploration stage had been accomplished in Spain in the 19th century. This was due to the development of the railroad on the Spanish tourism scenario. Also, these individuals who made incursions into Spain fell within the category of travelers and not tourists. This is why it can be deduced that it is the individual who is a traveler; although there may be exceptions, usually it is the visiting representative of the exploration stage. Such was the case of Penelope Chetwode and her sweet riding companion "Marquesa."

Even though travelling to this coastline for therapeutic saltwater treatments goes back in time to the year 1830, it is not until the 70's in this century, when a concerted effort was made to promote this Mediterranean space as a destination for international tourism. At this time, the construction of the first luxury hotels took place in Ronda and Algeciras, with the hope of attracting British nationals who had easy access to the region from Gibraltar.

Specifically, with the sponsorship of the British Consulate—and also it was understood, with the backing of the already numerous British colony residents in the province—an institution called the "Propagandistic Society for the Climate and Beautification of Málaga," was established in the city. With this information, being the highlight of tourism, during this period, it can be unquestionably affirmed that the exploration phase of the TALC theory had been completely attained by the last half of the19th century. The participation phase was about to become consolidated, through public and private investments and efforts.

THE PROMOTION AND CREATION OF TOURISM SECTOR INFRASTRUCTURE: THE PARTICIPATION PHASE

Spanish Regenerationism can find its temporal beginnings at the start of the 20th century. It was a movement rooted in the devastating loss of the remains of the Spanish empire, at the hands of the United States. Spanish philosophers and thinkers of the period reflected a spirit of decadence. It was thought that although Spain's economic forecast for the beginning of 1900 was not poor, it was underdeveloped compared to European northern countries.

Regenerationism gave birth to the first organized efforts, in 1905, to promote tourism. These efforts were translated into the founding of a small program, funded by a small budget, which was entitled, "The National Commission for the Promotion of Recreational and Artistic Excursions for the Foreign Public." This body became quite the novelty, as it was the first time that the word "tourism" was used in the title of a government institution, in Europe, placing Spain in the running for continental tourism development. It was understood that this sector was an economic resource, which had to be groomed and cultivated, at an integrated national level. To this end it was viewed as a means to incorporate the more backward regions into a general state of economic wellbeing.

Another organization replaced the former in 1911, called the "Royal Commissary of Tourism." These governmental interventions, in the development of the tourism sector, were very different from the "modus operandi" of that period, found in other Western European countries. This behavior was due more to the Spanish philosophy that public sponsorship, rather than private, was more effective.

Even though, World War I caused the tourism movement in Europe to lapse from 1914 through 1918 in Spain, government intervention in this economic sector once again, picked up speed with the Dictatorship of Primo de Rivera (1923-1930). With this political regime, yet another state organization was created to replace "The Royal Commissary of Tourism."

This newer entity was entitled "The National Board of Tourism." In the final analysis, it played more of a propagandistic role, than one of a true improvement of infrastructures. Though Primo de Rivera's liking of construction of massive public works, and improvements in infrastructure, so necessary for a fruitful development of this industry, led to an improvement of Spain's image as a viable tourist destination.

Another factor, which cannot be overlooked, was the fact that countries such as the U.S., France and Great Britain had legislated paid vacations by 1936. Also, Germany, with its fascist regime, had initiated a program of both foreign and national leisure, in order to increase the loyalty and patriotism of it citizens.

In consequence, it may be said that both the stages of exploration and participation were fully developed in the Costa del Sol during the beginnings of the 20th century, up until the Spanish Civil War, though there was a small period of stagnation during World War I.

Private travelers are the main motivators of the exploration phase. Both private and public entities are responsible for the participation and development stage. The difference between the Spanish exploratory and participation phases, and those defined by Butler, in other tourism destinations, is that the foreign tourist and the natives, do not have much contact with each other.

The rupture of this surge in Spanish tourism growth was caused by the Spanish Civil War, which began in 1936 and continued until 1939. This lack of tourism was compensated by the "Routes of War."

Holguin writes the following, regarding these routes:

> "The Nationalists beckoned European tourist to visit the "War Route of the North" while the Spanish Civil War was still in progress. Along with its messages targeting markedly different groups of people---those who wanted the authenticity of the battlefield experience and those who just wanted a relaxing scenic vacation...

This author continues:

> "The Spanish Nationalists began running organized tours of the recently secured northern front on July 1, 1938. They added a war route of the South through Andalucía in December of that same year.

And finally:

> "Collective known as the 'Rutas Nacionales de Guerra', these tours began every other day, between July 1 and October 1, in the northland, between December and April, in the south, until the end of World War II

This military tourism was the first in history where a regime that had not yet fully taken control of the government officially advertised itself as legitimate and sponsored this type of battlefield tourism. This "dark tourism" project had various purposes.

It can be said that the first and principal purpose was to provide the nationalist regime with sufficient revenue in order to continue with its battles. Reliable sources have ascertained that the nationalists collected more than seven million pesetas in profit, as it is calculated and recorded that between approximately 6,000 and 20,000 people visited the battlefields.

An additional goal accomplished by this wartime tourism was to legitimize the regime in the eyes of the international community. This was performed through the production of anti-republican propaganda, which portrayed the nationalists as a holy crusade or a religious recapturing of a culture. These tonalities and themes were projected, by the Franco regime to its citizens, as well as to the world, until the death of the dictator. It can be said, regarding the progression of the TALC, that during this period it was found to have regressed.

At the end of World War II, the Spanish government turned the development of the tourism industry to the private sector. During this global conflict, and even afterwards, the number of tourists visiting the "Routes of War" had decreased. Now, some still did venture to visit, though they were mainly substituted by Spanish tourists, but to a lesser degree. These Spaniards wanted to witness, first hand, the dimensions of the conflict on their native soil.

It can be affirmed that there was a lapse in beach tourism, which was a consequence of both the civil, as well as international, wars. This stage of the "Routes of War" reflects the stage of exploration. This is evident, as said stage is defined by small groups of tourists who follow irregular visiting patterns. This definition supplies the actual reality of that time, portrayed by the picture of Chrysler buses, following fixed routes through the military battlefields.

Accordingly, it can be said that this tourism is also related to the participation phase. This particular phase defines lodging as to be exclusively intended for visitors. Also, following this same concept, a form of publicity exists in order to attract tourist, and as has already been discussed, these visits are seasonal. It can also be noted that the government is taking the first steps in controlling the organization of this industry.

The exposure of tourists to natives in the previous cycles that have already been discussed, and that occurring, during the "Routes of War," is very limited. This is the only characteristic which does not adjust to Butler's analytical cycle of the TALC. Thus, this prevents the Spain of that time from only partially completing the exploration and participation cycles.

After World War II, tourism travel decreased in general as European economies, as well as with the aid of the American economy, were devoted to reconstruction. Spain was at a particular juncture. In that way, Spain was segregated by the United Nations, as well as from the economic aid the U.S. made to the devastated continent, due to war, in the form of the Marshall plan.

This segregation was due to the fact that Spain had become an ally of "The Axis," during World War II, and had signed the Anti-Comintern Pact with Italy and

Germany in 1939. Though, Spain never became, practically, aligned with them, nor did it ever enter into open hostilities with Great Britain or the United States, its pro-fascists stance during this time led to Spain's isolation with regard to the rest of Western Europe and the U.S.

However, this cold isolation towards Spain, a country that represented less of a threat than the Soviet Union, soon received a warmer, though still tepid, handshake from these countries, when the U.S.S.R was at the zenith of its power in the beginning of the 50's and at the height of the Cold War.

The West's attitude was to consider the Franco dictatorship as "the lesser of two evils." The dictatorship's policy, taking its cue from the West, was to form strong alliances with these western powers, project an image of modernity, but above all, one of anti-communism. This fortunate set of timing and circumstance, led to the acceptance of Spain, to the United Nations, and to its economic recuperation. Now, this country was set on maintaining a viable and secure place on the prosperous global stage.

Franco's policy of rapprochement was truly needed as Spain was totally poverty-stricken, and, thus, in great need of investment and cash currency. To this end, a courtship with American tourists was developed as dollar carrying visitors. Rosendorf comments to this effect:

> "...the Franco regime was strongly encouraged in the years following World War II's end to look to American tourism's potential economic propaganda benefits to Spain by prominent players within the U.S. travel and tourism industries, including American Express, Hilton Hotels, Trans-World Airlines, and Temple Fielding, the most popular American travel writer in the early post-war period.

Rosendorf continues along these same lines:

> Additionally, American motion picture producers who sought to make Hollywood films in Spain---foremost among them Samuel Bronston, producer of the epic El Cid, came to be seen, by the Franco regime as significant assets to Spain's tourism's policies, because of both the widespread distribution of attractive images of Spain and the glamour of Hollywood film production in the country.

And, finally, Rosendorf concludes:

> "The result was a potent synergy between American travel, tourism and entertainment business entrepreneurship, and Spanish travel, tourism, entertainment business entrepreneurship and Spanish political-economic ambitions in an altered international relations environment."

Before the Spanish Civil War, Spain was a country visited little, if not at all, by Americans. Although there is no official data to this effect, it is estimated that three or four thousand upper middle-class tourists from this country arrived yearly, principally to Spanish ports on board cruise ships (American Express 1940). However, these arrivals decreased due to the destruction caused by the Civil War, and the consequences thereof.

It was believed that Franco's secret police, in certain cases, maintained surveillance on the visitors. Their status was also ambivalent due to the exit and entrance visa requirements for their visit. In general, the regime projected a xenophobic mentality towards the arrival of foreigners.

Even though these visitors were tourists, according to the definition, in its strict sense, these arrivals found themselves in the situation of being travelers. The Spanish government continued to make plans to improve tourism infrastructure. However, the treasury never had sufficient funding to fulfill these necessary investments.

Even though, since the beginning of World War II, the intent was to extend credit, to both the private and public sectors, in order to have hotels built, and for the conservation of parks and beaches. This theory did not translate into practice, making this country's circumstances, as well as the tourism experience deplorable. These tourists, became but travelers, in the exploration phase.

No company was as important, for the Spanish tourism industry, as was American Express. This company had an historical working relationship with this country that dates back to April in 1921, until the present. While the importance of American tourism grew throughout the decade of the 50's, it can be affirmed that the stages of exploration and participation were completed. The development phase is only partially completed, however. Therefore, it can be observed that the Torremolinos municipality on the Costa del Sol duplicated its number of edifications between 1950 and 1960 (Pollard and Domínguez Rodríguez, 1995).

THE DEVELOPMENT PHASE IN THE COSTA DEL SOL

With the arrival of the decade of the 60's, tourism from Northern Europe to the Costa del Sol began to rebound, by comparison with that from the transatlantic. At the same time, this region recovered its prosperity. Therefore, around 1960, European tourism, in Spain had multiplied by tenfold while that from America, only by three.

The Caudillo himself recognized the importance of tourism upon his arrival in Málaga, where he gave a speech for the inauguration of a hotel and spoke of its relevance for the national economic future. This speech was a total game changer, as a decade earlier, in the same city, Franco had forecast that the capital of the Costa del Sol would be an industrial center, in which its beautiful blue skies would be darkened by the smoke from its factory's chimneys. As a result of this policy, there was even greater tourism development.

As indicated by Pollard and Dominguez:

"...by the mid-1960's 'popular' hotels and the first apartments would appear. 'The Pez Espada,' in common with the general tone of Torremolinos at that time, was a luxury hotel in the 5-star category."

These authors continue:

> "This emphasis continued into the early 1960's, but beginning to appear with the advent of the package tour, while Marbella made its first inroads into usurping Torremolinos' up-market position with the Club Naútico and marina at Puerto Banús."

They also write to this effect:

> "Overall, some 7,970 beds were provided in 21 hotels built during the 1960's, bringing about a vast expansion of the resort. In particular, much of the land between La Carihuela and the main road was filled with the expansion invading neighboring Benalmádena."

In that way, it can be said that a tourism boom took place from the 60's to the present. During this time, Fraga Iribarne must be mentioned, as the Minister of Information and Tourism from 1962 to 1968. With the aging of the dictator, he was a noteworthy figure, in that he was able to arrive at a more independent development and direction of the Spanish tourism industry. Under Fraga's stewardship, the slogan, "Spain is Different" was created. However, paradoxically, Spain was no longer "different" from the rest of Europe, once the tourism invasion began. This incursion peaked in the 70's, with a brief interruption due to the petroleum crisis from 1973 to 1974.

During this time, it can be said that the exploration, participation and development phases were completed. This last phase was accomplished primarily through private investment and in an anarchical fashion. The legislation, which controlled the development of this period, was that of the Law of Urban Land and Order of 1956. However, it contained many judicial loopholes, as with its application, it was possible to manipulate the definitions of urban and rural land.

Also, the supreme authority that supposedly had oversight regarding municipal planning did not function accordingly, or had yet to be created. There were also complaints from the Costa del Sol, as well as from the Costa Brava, that both entities were burdened with all costs, while the profits went to benefit the coffers of the impoverished central region of Castille. Municipalities such as Torremolinos lacked in revenue due to the taxation policy imposed upon them. Therefore, they found themselves unable to accomplish their own urban planning goals. In this way, these goals fell into the hands of private investors. This period can be defined by the following activity:

> "The 1980's began with another recession, but the period 1985 to 1988 saw a sharp jump in tourist travel to Spain, with the number of visitors increasing from 43 million to 54 million. As the price of the tourist product also increased markedly over this period, Spanish receipts from tourism doubled"

And these authors continue to state:

"Torremolinos briefly shared in this bonanza, and 1985-1987 showed the second largest expansion in building since the tourist boom began."

From the 60's to the 70's, the tourism market targeted clientele with low purchasing power. Charter flights, in many cases with retired World War II pilots at the controls, brought the visitors to enjoy the triple pleasures of "sea, sun and sand." They would find lodging, in cheap hotels, where the meals were served "buffet" style, in order to economize.

Now, in the post-Franco era, the phases of exploration, participation, development and consolidation have all been completed. It can be said that the development phase has been completed, in the Costa del Sol, as there are extensive publicity campaigns, in order to attract tourists to the region. Also, change in the physical appearance, may be noted, as well, such as the construction of new hotel buildings, amusement parks, apartment buildings and golf courses.

It can be proven, by the same token, that the consolidation phase is complete. This has occurred as the increase of relative numbers of tourists has declined, though the absolute numbers continue to increase. If too many people crowd a destination, that may put it at risk for future lack of attraction in the future, as Navarro Jurado indicated in his study.

It is foreseeable that efforts may be made in order to extend the tourist season. A noticeable discontent may be noted among the residents, given the pressures the tourism impact creates in this society. This has already taken place in certain segments of the population of the Costa del Sol, given the insatiable gluttony of water caused by the golf courses.

In 1975, a legislative body was superimposed on the previously mentioned 1956 legislation. It was entitled the Reform of the Urban Land and Order Law. It recognized the management problems, in the theoretical body of its legislative predecessor, but remained unsuccessful in practice. In the hope of overcoming the past, and incorporating the democratic spirit of the time, in 1983, The General Order Plan for Málaga was proclaimed. This legislative body can be described in the following manner:

"This second Málaga municipal plan thus contained provisions for environmental conservation and protection as well as restating the land zonation policy of earlier abortive legislation where by categories of urban, urbanisable (urban reserve), and non-urbanisable (rural) land were recognized and provisions were made for economic and social infrastructures.

They finalize, by saying, in this regard:

"Despite such admissions and good intentions, the development-oriented mentality so evident up to 1975 continued in the post-Franco era in Málaga/ Torremolinos, as it did in other parts of Spain."

TOWARDS A CONSOLIDATION OR TRANSITION PHASE?

It can be said that, currently, the Costa del Sol has entered into a stagnation or "pre-stagnation" phase stage, devised by this book, given the particular characteristics of the region. As it has been proven in this Chapter, this destination has, historically, gone through all the other phases. This can be stated given the fact that the carrying capacity of the variables of some of its resources has been reached, or even overtaken, its most basic structures. Most noteworthy is the region's consumption of this scarce and necessary resource, water.

It should, also be noted that this stage is characterized, at the same time, by repeat tourism. Regarding this phenomenon of repeating visitors, this astounding figure has been advanced of 600 thousand English-speaking tourists, living in Southern Spain in 1999. Also, astounding was the figure of 25,000 British citizens, who were found to be residing in Mijas, which is a village of only 36,000 inhabitants.

O'Reilly formulated the following classification:

> "...three main groups among the British in Spain, the residents, the visitors and the tourists. But the migrant groups are subdivided thus:
>
> - Full Residents,
> - Returning Residents,
> - Seasonal Visitors, and
> - Peripatetic Visitors."

This information adds to the idea of a "Northern Invasion," with the existence of two categories: that of travelers and that of tourists, which are similar, in many cases to a migration. This conceptual body represents those that repeatedly visit the Costa del Sol, or who already live there, permanently. For such a specific categorization to exist suggests that the Costa del Sol is, effectively, in the stagnation stage.

In conclusion, it could, also be argued that the Costa del Sol has entered into the Rejuvenation phase, while skipping the decline phase, delineated in the TALC. This can be said because the appetite and taste for the triple "S's," sea, sun, and sand are a constant throughout time, as long as the infrastructure of necessary resources is maintained adequately. This has occurred at Niagara Falls, and the same thing seems to be occurring, in the Costa del Sol. Definitively, there are at least rays of hope for this tourist destination.

To begin with, plans for the rejuvenation of the place have been translated into a judicial body, with new legislation regulating urbanizable land. Regarding its natural resources, and at a more pragmatic level, sewage water treatment plants have been established along the coastline. In terms of the golf course that consume seemingly unlimited quantities of water, but which also have the purpose of diversifying the tourism supply, water recycling plants have been installed to water these courses. This technology, thus, relieves the impact and stress, on the aquatic resources of the region. There is garbage collection, where waste is recycled. Also, there are political policies in place to reduce noise contamination, as well as swimming water contamination in the municipalities of the region.

If the premise that the Costa del Sol is in the rejuvenation stage of its life cycle is or is not accepted, what cannot be denied is that Spain is no longer "different," as its yesteryear publicity slogan once touted. Due to the consolidation of its tourism industry, this nation now belongs to the family of the most industrialized and modern countries of the West. Upon finding itself, in this economic cycle of its national and regional reality, now, this country is facing those corresponding problems of that phase. For the benefit of its population—be they natives, residents or tourists—Spain must find solutions to its dilemmas, also be they ecological, economical, or social, meeting the challenges, as has been its character, historically, to do so.

CHAPTER 7

The Life Cycle Theory of a Tourism Area and the Influence of Physical Geography on the Costa del Sol

This chapter presents the geographical surroundings of the area that is studied, that is the Western Costa del Sol, or the Costa del Golf, as it has also been called. Here, the purpose is to establish the background of the physical elements of the surroundings, such as climate, topography, vegetation and hydrology.

Reference is also made to the Mediterranean Sea and its beaches, given the fact that the surge in the industry of tourism is due to the region's warm climate and location on the coast of said sea. These all represent attractions for the market of European countries that export tourists.

Here, internal factors are discussed, such as the intensification of water usage, as well as external issues, such as climate change, which has altered those conditions. The intent is to showcase the region's vulnerability, as it faces changes in environmental conditions, which might suggest changes in the visitation patterns to the space.

THE INFLUENCE OF CLIMATE IN THE CONSTITUTION OF THE COSTA DEL SOL, AS A TOURIST DESTINATION

Regarding climate in Europe, there are three main existing sources which affect the continent: the Arctic Seas in the North, the Atlantic Ocean in the West, the land mass of Eurasia in the East, and to the South, the Sahara Desert, as well as most importantly, the Mediterranean Sea. The sources of continental tropical air originate in the Sahara Desert. They have a great influence in the Mediterranean because they contribute to long and dry summers, and in general, the existence of warm winters, along the Spanish Costa del Sol.

The Mediterranean climate and Western European climate, in general, are affected by these western winds. The tropical sea air acquires its humidity and warmth as it sets over the Gulf of Mexico. This tropical marine air is extended throughout the Atlantic Ocean, in a northwestern direction, as it mixes and joins forces with the Gulf current. This combination brings warm and humid conditions to Western Europe, and to a lesser degree to Central Europe. This tropical sea air, as well as the marine currents, suffer a cooling down process, as they penetrate further into Central Europe. However, this air retains its warm temperature as it arrives to the continental west.

The weather of the north Atlantic varies seasonally. In the winter, bordering between the tropical marine air and the polar sea air, depressions are formed which move towards the west. This brings rain, and even cold winters, as well as snow to Europe. The marine polar air acquires its characteristics above the Arctic Ocean. This cool and humid air arrives to Western and Central Europe from the north and north east region of the continent.

This air mass is characterized by its instability. Upon touching land, it is quickly pushed upwards, and may produce rain, showers, hale, or snow, depending on the season. This polar air mass usually makes its appearance during winter months. During this season, the polar front, which is the initial edge of the cool Arctic air, is found to the south of the continent. Though it too, may be located, in the north, in the summer, and cause an abnormally cool season.

However, anomalies in air current movements do occur. For example, though they may not break any records, summers sometimes see unusually cool temperatures, as the Arctic current of air is steered towards the south of the European continent, throughout the meteorological season. By contrast, warmer and drier summers may take place when the Arctic current is kept to the north of Western Europe.

Therefore, the climatological phenomenon in Europe is complex. The so-called Atlantic Transmitting Ribbon, or the Atlantic Thermohaline, is at risk of no longer functioning. If this occurs, Greenland's temperatures could fall. This would have disastrous consequences for Europe, as this marine current is what keeps Europe from freezing temperatures during winter. Among these climatological events, prolonged droughts might take place in certain regions, while heavy precipitation may be found in others.

In spite of the cooler temperatures in the summer of 2004, the spring of 2005 (See Chart V) experimented a smaller average of rainfall than normal. Already in the month of July, the Costa del Sol was on the alert for restrictions of water supply. Along with this lack of water, an extreme heat wave that affected the entire peninsula was experienced. In the south, pasturelands, brush and undergrowth caught fire due to the summer heat. Crops were unable to be harvested and cattle were lost in the destruction. Sometimes the climatic variability can work in favor of an area, as Spain received the much-needed rainfall at the end of that month. Experts (Blouet 2007) were convinced that the air currents following very unusual patterns due to global warming.

However, normally in summer and in Southern Spain, the winds usually blow from the south from the Sahara Desert. This air crosses the Mediterranean, where it receives humidity. It can be so warm in the months of July and August that it may cause discomfort to the residents of the interior or of the coast. This mass of semi-desert air is called the "Leveche," in Southern Spain.

However, generally temperately warm Mediterranean climate, with long and dry, as well as hot, summers, is what predominates in this space. Winters are tempered and short, perfect for playing golf. However, the geographic relief of the area, such as the Sierra Nevada, and the Bética Mountains give way to climatological variations.

At any rate, phenomenon, such as climate change, can affect this Spanish coastline, causing its beaches to disappear (Chanton 2002). The Mediterranean Sea, as its name indicates, means "in the middle of land," which being a plus for the area, could now become a negative threat, as the sea absorbs and swallows the shoreline, along with its beaches. This could happen as the ice of polar caps melts and

Greenland's glaciers decrease in size (at approximately eight kilometers per year) at a speed two times more quickly than what had originally been predicted.

The paradox can be found, in the fact that the creative forces of all wealth that stimulated the tourism industry, that is to say the industrial revolution can be the cause of tourism's fading into twilight. This irrational exploitation of natural resources, with the increasing growth of contaminants in the environment, is a motivating force, not only of the demise of tourism, but also of life on the entire planet.

According to NASA, and other organizations that kept records to this effect, 2016 was the hottest year ever registered, in the Northern Hemisphere. The temperature has increased on average by 0.8 degrees Celsius since 1980, and two thirds of this warming has occurred since 1975, at the rate of approximately 0.15-0.20 degrees per decade. If this continues, the Costa del Sol's advantageous position as a beach destination could be threatened.

The following has been written regarding the effects of climate change on the Mediterranean:

> "This global trend will not fail to have considerable repercussions on the Mediterranean climate, which could occur rather rapidly during the coming decades, but it is scarcely possible at present to define their exact nature. It is fairly widely accepted that with an average temperature increase of 1.5 C in the temperature by 2025 the region will experience a cyclonic shift to the north, which will affect its central and western areas in winter.[141]

These authors continue, along the same lines of thought: "In these areas rainfall would continue to depend heavily on relief and would be higher in the north, but conversely, areas of uncertain rainfall in the south could spread and evapotranspiration would be everywhere.[142]

Finally, they forecast:

> "It goes without saying that a change of this kind would have serious consequences, notably for agriculture and the hydrological regime. Ensuing changes in the thermal structure of water bodies could also produce modification in marine currents in the region."[143]

Therefore, without assuming an alarmist position, it can be estimated that the availability of water resources will decrease, as will water power, which has already become a problem (*El economista* online 2007). This climate change will also affect the tourism capacity of the area, aside from the production of crops. As has already been discussed and proven historically, as well, there may be health risks, which affect human lives due to heat waves increasing the danger of forest fires.

---

[141] Michael Grennon and Michel Batisse, *Futures for the Mediterranean Basin: The Blue Plan* (Oxford: Oxford University Press, 1989), 6.

[142] *Ibid.* pp. 6.

[143] *Ibid.* pp. 6.

The cause of this phenomenon has been discussed in the following terms:

> "But most important of all, a prospective study has to mention the possible trend of world climate towards heating up, due to the 'greenhouse effect' caused by the accumulation of carbon dioxide and other industrial gases such as freons (CFC's) and methane in the atmosphere."[144]

Grenon and Batisse continue, in this way: "It will take several years of study before definite and accurate indications are available concerning the extent of the greenhouse effect and its consequences in the various regions of the world."[145]

Regarding global temperature increases, these authors calculate the following: "It is generally admitted that the average temperature throughout the world could rise by 0.5 C to 2 C by 2030, and 3.5 C by 2050, which is a considerable change compared to the historical past."[146]

These scientists finally conclude, factoring the role inertia plays in climate change: "Moreover, even if all carbon dioxide and CFC emissions were stopped today, inertia would cause a warming up of the planet in any event, because of the amounts already accumulated in the atmosphere"[147]

Also, the Costa del Sol's geographic proximity to tourist exporting countries, the Mediterranean climate, conditioned by the air of the African desert, along with the practice of golf, anchored in its numerous courses, have all been factors, which have allowed this coastline to become this new market segment's preferred destination. To this end, the British, the Germans and other European nationals throng to this region to play this sport, when the climate of their own homelands is too inhospitable for its practice.

It is interesting to note, however, that the demand for the golf courses or their "green fees," typically has decreased during the winter months in recent times in the Costa del Sol (spoken interview with Juan Cantos in June, 2007, director of the Río Real Monteros golf course, Marbella). This fall, in the number of golfers during this period, can be attributed to climate change.

This is due to the fact that countries such as Great Britain and Germany that typically experience harsh winters, so inappropriate for the practice of this sport, are experiencing a rise in their winter temperatures. This prolonged period of warmer weather is allowing golfers to spend more time in their native lands for the practice of this sport. Thus, the need to travel to the Costa del Sol to take advantage of the region's warm winters, in order to play golf has been reduced.

On the other hand, the environmental pressure that this conglomeration of golf courses, built on the "Costa del Golf," is exerting on the area is very concerning, at best. In order to regulate this activity, as well as its water usage, a decree began to formulate in 2004 and was completed in 2006. The Councils on the Environment, Public Works, and Tourism and Sports participated in its formulation.

---

[144] *Ibid.* pp. 26.
[145] *Ibid.* pp. 26.
[146] *Ibid.* pp. 26.
[147] *Ibid.* pp. 26.

The principal precept in this piece of legislation, was to separate the courses from the housing developments, with the explicit prohibition to construct any more housing. The population of the Province of Málaga, in 2003, was 900,000 inhabitants (though, at present, its capital city is just a little over half a million). The potential supply of water was sufficient for only 1.1 million inhabitants. (Navarro Jurado 2003). Facing this dire situation, solutions were sought out on the various drafts. Some exceptions were allowed, as long as the housing developments were small.

Also, they had to be located at a minimum distance from the golf courses and involve a low density of construction. If hotels were permitted to be built, they also had to have a low-density design. The stipulations were a maximum of a construction of three floors, and capacity for 300, in the case of an 18-hole golf course, and a capacity of 400, for a 27-hole installation. Perhaps, the most important inclusion in this decree was the imposition of the need to use recycled water for the watering of the courses.

Global warming may be a threat to civilization, as it stands, and how we perceive it, at present. The efforts which are being made in the Costa del Sol to regulate the situation created by the golf courses, and thereby to reduce the vulnerability of the aquatic resources, may be difficult to accomplish. However, the consequence of inaction, in this sense, would prove to be even more threatening, as they would likely involve the survival of the lifestyle of the Costa del Sol, as it is known today.

From that point it may be deduced that the environmental conditions are decisive for the Costa del Sol as a tourism destination. This can be said especially in the case of the establishment of golf courses, which depend on atmospheric variations, and an abundance of water, in order to maintain the greenness of their grass. (Pérez 12/28/2007 *El país*).

TOPOGRAPHIC ASPECTS: THE IMPORTANCE OF THE PHYSICAL SURROUNDINGS

Aside from the phenomenon of climate change, the topography contributes to affect the climate of the region. However, its incidence on the social activity of the resident is less discernible. This is because human beings develop and interpret their physical surroundings in a relative way, doing so independently of the obstacles presented by climate or topography.

The Béticas Mountains are found in the Costa del Sol. Their name is of Roman origin, La Baética. These mountains enclose the Guadalquivir Valley to the south. These are composed of stones, which were formed in a much more recent geological era than that of the central plains of the Iberian Peninsula. Their peaks rise to altitudes much higher than those of the central sierras.

The Béticas Mountains are truly divided into two parallel strips of hills, separated by a long and narrow depression, called the Intrabética. This is known in the province of Málaga as the Hoyo de Antequera. The Seranía de Ronda is to the west. The mountain ranges with the highest peaks are those of Almijara, Tejeda and Alhma, which are found toward the east. The strip, which is found to the furthermost south and parallel to that of Ronda is the Sierra of Bermeja, which boasts of the roughest and sharpest decline.

These Bética mountains extend from Gibraltar towards the north east to Cabo Nao, for a distance of approximately 700 kilometers. They are cut into short segments of hills at certain points, as they are traversed by valleys. The tallest of these mountains is the Sierra Nevada. This peak is snow-covered all year long. The highest point of the Sierra Nevada is Mulhacén, which reaches a height of approximately 6,000 meters.

The Bética Sierras are located very close to the Mediterranean Sea. They only allow for a narrow coastline, where the villages of the Costa del Sol are nestled. These mountains block the cooler air from the central plain and from the Sierra Nevada. They also keep the desert air from the Sahara in a geographical position, allowing for warm and short winters, a micro-climate perfect for the development of the game of golf.

THE ENDEMIC FLORA

The flora of the Costa del Sol has suffered historically, due to burning, sacrificing it for the sake of agriculture, since the times of the Romans. The introduction of the goat has altered the vegetation of the place as well. More recently, the land has been submitted to fertilizers and pesticides, leaving it early on with an uncared for degraded aspect, due to human activity. The plants of the region, aside from their manipulation by man, have had to adapt to almost simultaneous periods of heat and drought, common to Mediterranean climate. Also, the species have varied in the last millennium, not necessarily because of their adaptation to the environment, but because of the needs and dispositions of human beings. At the same time, the following must be taken into consideration:

> "…during recent centuries many plants were introduced into the Mediterranean, area suited by its climate to shrub crops. Some species are suited for human consumption (olive, fig, pomegranate, orange, tomato, aubergine, maize etc.), others to industry (eucalyptus, acacia etc.) others to landscaping (bougainvillea, palm etc.)."[148]

The explanation is thus, given that: "These species were originated in other parts of the world and have now become so well adapted to the region, that it is easily forgotten that they were once foreign to it."[149]

The vegetation that is native to the region is, primarily, shrub land, where the palmetto is the most representative. In the Sierra of the Snows, the Spanish Fur and pines thrive. In the interior of the area forests of oak and cork oak are found. All this vegetation must be guarded in order to conserve it, as all this coastal land, as well as

---

[148] *Ibid.* pp. 9.
[149] *Ibid.* pp. 9

that of the Mediterranean in general, is very fragile and vulnerable, as well as sensible to any physical or chemical degradation that it may suffer.

This fragility has been accented with the overwhelming presence of the golf courses, which imply the cutting down of trees and the destruction of much vegetation, to be replaced by large extensions of areas of green grass. This has motivated protests from ecological groups against the construction of more golf courses. These groups say that these golfing spaces destroy the natural flora and fauna of the place.

However, some golf courses, such as La Cala in Mijas, promotes itself as being a protector of the environment. In its magazine published in the summer of 2007, a photograph was published with a note that touted the progress that was being made in the construction of its roads and infrastructure:

> "During the work great care was taken to protect all the indigenous trees that had to be removed. Twenty-three Cork Oak trees were transplanted from the development areas to the 7th and 17th holes of Campo Europa."[150]

THE HYDROGRAPHY: THE IMPACT OF WATER ON THE TOURISM SECTOR

With reference to the hydrography, the Costa del Sol has been included within "Dry Spain" (See Graph V, Map II). That is, it belongs to the area of a level of rainfall that is below the national average. The irony can also be found in that this is the area that, at the same time, has a great consumption of water, due to its growing popularity, which has been on the rise, since the 60's as a tourist destination.

With the intent of widening, as well as diversifying its tourist market, over 83 golf courses have been built from Málaga to Cádiz, with numerous housing developments, where crystal clear pool waters glisten in the sun light, and carefully manicured lawns, only increase the consumption of this extremely scarce resource.

These residential and sporting edifications place enormous pressure on the aquatic resources of the area. In Marbella specifically, the consumption of water per inhabitant was above the national mean. In Málaga proper, 27 percent more of this precious liquid is consumed above the national average. The consumption of water increases but the supply of rain water from mother nature does not increase at the same speed. Logically, in dry years, more irrigation is necessary than in wetter years, and thus, more pressure during these times is placed on the water reserves. (See Graphs VI, VII and VIII for comparison).

Marbella has more than 33 square kilometers of golf courses. Each thirsty square meter consumes 10 liters of drinking water a day during the high season. However, it is maintained that recycled water would be an alternative to this break-neck speed of consumption, yet it is said that because of its high content of nitrate and sodium it damages the grass. It also smells poorly, and this odor is disagreeable to the golfers. (Interview maintained with Juan Campos op. cit.).

---

[150] La Cala Resort Newsletter, Summer 2007, (26).

Here, it is possible to define the possibilities of the uses of recycled water and to define what the recycling process entails. The exact definition of recycling means to recover useful materials from garbage or waste. It can also mean to extract or utilize something again. This term is usually used with reference to newspaper, aluminum cans and glass jars, but it can also be related to water. A common form of recycled water is that which comes from municipal sewage dumping. Its terminology is synonymous to reutilization or reclamation.

Nature is the main and oldest recycler of water. However, this process normally refers to a technological project, which accelerates this procedure, and has been accomplished, naturally on the planet for millions of years. In this way, the process can be divided into planned operations and unplanned operations. A planned recycled system would be that of treatment of waters, which have already been utilized by a population upstream and which are received by a population downstream. These projects have the goal of reutilizing a supply of recycled water for the benefit of society.

The level of water treatment is a function of human exposure to it. If this resource is not sufficiently treated, it could cause sicknesses, as it is a carrier of bacteria and contaminants, which can threaten human health.

The treatment phases are the following:

1. "Primary treatment (sedimentation). It is a process by which use is made of gravitational pull, to allow solid material to float to the top or fall to the bottom. Then they are extracted.

2. Secondary treatment (biological treatment). Bacteriological organisms are used to digest dissolved organic material, as well as small particles that are too small to settle. In the measure that these bacteria eat and grow, they convert the water into a component that is, at least, 95% pure.

3. Advanced treatment: A filter composed of many layers of sand and charcoal are used to purify any particle that was left in the liquid from the previous stage. Chlorine is added in this state in order to kill all bacteria, viruses, and other pathogenic organisms. In this stage, the water is at a 99% state of purification. At this time, it exceeds or equals many drinking water standards.

4. Treatment of Recycled Water: A reduplication of parts of an organism is used, in order to lessen the total amount of dissolved solids. The liquid is then, filtered through another filter of various layers. "[151]

---

[151] "Water Recycling and Reuse: The Environmental Benefits," EPA website, accessed April 8, 2007 http://www.epa.gov/region09/water/recycling/.

Recycled water is not usually for direct drinking water purposes, but rather, its usage is confined to agriculture, gardening, irrigation, and for golf course watering. For the latter, the water only needs to be treated at the secondary level. For agriculture, recycled water contains more nutrients, and therefore, less prejudicial fertilizers to the environment are required.

Other drinking applications can be used in the industry, such as for water cooling generators, for the production of electricity or oil refineries. It can also be used in paper mills, for carpet dying, and in the functioning of domestic toilets. It is useful too, in construction as a cement mixer. In nature, artificial lakes are filled with recycled water.

The indirect reutilization of drinking water refers to projects that discharge water into an aquatic body before reusing it. The direct utilization is for the explicit use as drinking water. The majority of recycled water is not used for this direct drinking usage in Spain, nor in the U.S. In that case, the indirect reutilization is preferably used. That is to say, the water bearing subterranean resources are recharged with this resource, so that salt water will not intrude in the coastal areas, and the dammed water surfaces are increased. The direct drinking water system is more well-known and is more successful in Namibia, Africa (Ibid. EPA).

Another problem is that, in the Costa del Sol, the cost of water still remains low when compared to other European countries. In Marbella, a cubic meter per consumer has a price of only 2.2 euros a month in 2016, while in Great Britain, the average cost of water in 2010 was 50 Sterling Pounds per month. The low price of this resource is an environmental issue considered by ecologists, owners and public administrators alike. If there is not an economic mechanism that encourages the demand to decrease, this factor can only be expected to increase. Another confusing point, in this regard, is that private consumers' water usage is, generally, generated on community meters, in which case, the customer's consumption does not reflect what he or she pays (Pérez 2006 op. cit.).

Unfortunately, the Reservoir La Concepión only has a limited capacity (See Chart I), as determined by the public water company, ACOSOL, and, specifically, according to the information provided by it Chief Head of Sanitation Planning, Pedro Muñoz Luque. The pressure on this damn and all other waterways is notorious during the months of drought. These levels become alarmingly low in the summer months when rainfall is slight. During this season, not only is the reservoir empty but also the rivers run dry. During a research study performed on site, for this publication, it was observed that in July 2009, the Tortuga, Guadalmina (where a golf course and housing development were located), Guadarrama, Valerín, Padrón, Guadalabón and Manilva riverbeds were entirely dry. Also, the Emedio, Vaquero, Jordano, Gualquitón, and De la Mujer were also completely parched.

This drought regarding the river systems of the area can affect the nutrition of the sand on the beaches, as the rivers are the sediment carriers, according to certain sources. However, the late Derek Danta, (verbal interview, 2007) refutes this theory. To this effect, he said the following:

"A decrease in the water table will not, adversely, affect the transporting of sand to the beaches. The lack of river system activity can impact the particles, which are the size of mud or mud silt. The sand transportation will occur during winter storms."[152]

In general, Derek Danta considered the area of the Mediterranean to be one of low environmental energy.

However, even though the beaches do not suffer because of this lack of fluvial activity, the subject of resolving the issue of water consumption for tourists and residents is still at hand. The government approved the National Hydraulic Plan, on July 5th in October of 2001. Here, the strategy was to utilize water transfers. In 2004, a judicial order was introduced, through the Royal Decree of the 18th of June 2004, to enable the reutilization of resources. In other words, the tactic became to put measures into play that were more in harmony with the natural environment, as opposed to acting against it aggressively. This new philosophy can be considered as an improvement in policy.

A more radical position, though unofficial, is that of the ecologists, which falls into the ranks of the "Green Movement." This group existed even before the death of Franco. This faction shared similarities with the "Conservationist" movement, which existed in Eastern Europe under Communist regimes.

In his usual astute way, the dictator permitted these groups to carry on, under his watchful eye, as a pressure valve release. They did not directly criticize the regime, but mainly directed their efforts reputing the loss of flora and fauna, the deterioration of the environment and the damage the development of tourism was causing to the Spanish coastline.

These ecologists from the past, as well as their descendants of the present, view golf courses as globalized capitalistic models of destructive development. Currently, they propose small agricultural industries as an alternative to these sports structures. This group wants to include, in their project, the creation of ecologically friendly agricultural cooperatives, selling directly to the consumer. In this way, rural tourism would be developed with products of local origin.

ACOSOL, the local water agency, proposes an alternative, which is more in consonance with the already established, economic goals. It suggests regional initiatives, in order to minimize the scarcity of water. This is a public limited company, created by the Association of the Municipalities of the Costa de Sol. As indicated by Muñoz and Miranda. This company has the following functions:

1. Filtering and distribution of drinking water.
2. Desalinization of sea water.
3. Pick-up, transportation and purification of sewage waters.
4. Distribution and supply of recycled water for watering.

---

[152] Interview Dr. Derek Danta, late Dean of School of Social and Behavioral Sciences, California State University, Northridge, October 2007.

5. Gutter servicing.[153]

In their paper, these authors make a strong plea for the reutilization of water resources given the great urban growth of the area, which, of course, implies an increase in its consumption. Also, well water is being drained, which is caused by the pressure put on them by the golf courses and their housing developments. It is estimated that an average 18-hole golf course consumes the same amount of water as an urban center of 15,000 people. This is not counting the pools and other infrastructure, which feed off of these sports installations. The golf courses diminish the water consumption in cities, as well as that of the aquatic reserves. Also, it should be considered that sea water intrudes into wells when their ground is lost.

Regarding the region of Andalucía, there are more than a total of 104 golf courses, which exist in its area. According to Pedro Muñoz Luque, Chief Head of Sanitation Planning of ACOSOL, 50 percent of them are in the province of Málaga, and over 40 percent are in the Costa del Sol, nestled in golf resorts and housing developments of high water consumption. (see Graph IV). Fortunately, over 35 percent of these use recycled water from ACOSOL, and the number is growing. Also, many more are projected to be joined to this water recycling network, though at a high cost (See Graph II). It is predicted that in the foreseeable future, as many as 20 new golf courses will join the system of recycled water.

However, according to a telephone interview, conducted with Pedro Muñoz Luque in February 2018, it was revealed that there are still courses that receive recycled water, yet they continue to mix it with well water. Nonetheless, under his direction, ACOSOL, continues to forge ahead with new plans for future networks of water purification systems, with which to network golf courses. (See Graph III).

This partial or complete dependence on well water must end and regulations, such as the Drought Decree, must be complied with and obeyed. This decree does not establish water reductions for domestic consumption, but it does reduce the consumption by 15% and to 230 liters per inhabitant by day. However, this measure does not allow for sumptuary uses, such as hosing off the streets, car washing outside of authorized establishments, garden watering, or the functioning of ornamental fountains, without a closed water circuit, as well as the filling of both private and public pools. The former activities are found in numerous quantities in the housing within the golf course developments.

Upon forbidding all these uses, except for human consumption, it is understood that the purpose is to maintain the availability of water for the consumption of the population. The golf courses are forbidden from using drinking water for their irrigation and they are limited to a maximum of 200 cubic meters per acre/month of non-drinking water. The usage of this water, for this purpose, is a concession to the use of properly recycled water.

The complete utilization of recycled water for the irrigation of golf courses, not only benefits those of the present, but it will also be a benefit to those built in the

---

[153] P. Muñoz and E. Miranda, "Evolution and Problems of Recycled Water in Western Costa del Sol," Unpublished paper presented at The International Conference on Golf and the Environment, Roqueta, March 14 - 16, 2007, ACOSOL, Public Limited Company

future, as it will assure enough of this necessary resource for their development. By continuing with the efforts of water recycling to satisfy the needs of sports, the resources will recharge themselves by percolation, thereby allowing for more availability of water for other uses.

This is a method which has proven to be effective, in order to protect the environment, but will also lead to fewer confrontations with what are becoming feared ecologist groups. According to ACOSOL's figures, throughout 2006, 54, 80 Hm3 were filtered; 7.1 Hm3 were reutilized (1.3%). It is predicted that in the future, 24Hm3 will be reused, and with this reserve, a population of 270 inhabitants could be served (Muñoz P. Miranda E. 2007).

The future and present projections are not very encouraging for various reasons. On one hand, as has already been discussed, well water is still being misused. Although, there is a Drought Decree in existence, more comprehensive legislation is lacking. Water is a natural resource, which is comparable to, yet more important still, than coal or oil.

As it is found unequally distributed in nature, it is difficult to apply rigorous and structured regulations to it. Also, the recycling process is a procedure which requires resources, as well as qualified personnel, for its development. The need for necessary filters, in order to pick up and transport the water goes without saying, as well as is demonstrated by the accompanying graphs.

During the Franco era, the slogan "Spain is different" was coined. The irony of this phraseology, now lies in the fact that this "difference," which was so successfully advertised in this country to attract foreign visitors, soon transformed this space, into the common denominator of so many comparable tourist destinations. Its coast, so overexploited by this industry, very soon took on the look and appearance of many other coasts giving it a feeling of "placelessness." The Costa del Sol had lost its "difference."

Therefore, populated by towering apartment buildings and hotels, the Costa del Sol has lost its appeal. To this end, it has had to create artificial attractions, in order to maintain its place, in the national and international market. Golf courses have been added to these concrete masses, which do not belong to this coastline's natural environment. These courses represent a support to the tourist industry, given the character of their new newer and trendier appeal.

This support can be translated into greatly significant numbers for the Spanish gross national product, as it represents at least six percent of it. Though their financial success for the nation still cannot take away the damage they cause to the environment. This especially occurs in "Dry Spain" where these courses continue to deplete this scarce resource. (See Chart V and Map II)

In this way, the esthetics of the coastline has been lost, but also recently, tourists have lost their trust in the cleanliness of the Mediterranean and of its beaches. It is important to emphasize the word "recently," because the identification of the standards of the quality of the beaches and water continually fluctuate according to the discoveries and advances made in modern science.

Recently, for example, importance has begun to be given to viruses as an active component of sand or in the water that covers it. For a very long time, there has been an awareness regarding the threats of bacteria and other pathogens. The presence of these is due to large amount of sewage, which is dumped into the sea water. Also, until very recently, the control of deposits of toxic components in swimming water left much to be desired. The principal source of the sewage, as well as of the toxic compounds, comes from the urban centers, as well as river mouths.

For the long term, it is still unknown what the effect of the toxins produced by industries in the coastal cities or in rivers upstream will be. What can be stated is that the dumping of sewage in the sea, which borders the Costa del Sol is seasonal, and increases during the summer months, when there is a large producing population of this substance.

The condition of the water and the sand worsens, given that the Mediterranean Sea barely has a tide, to speak of, as well as very few currents. It can almost be described as a big bathtub. To make matters worse, a current of water from the Atlantic has an inlet through the Strait of Gibraltar, but no outlet. In its favor, it can be said that along its coastline the Mediterranean has very few river mouths.

In any case, compared to the Atlantic or Pacific Oceans—or to any more powerful or choppier bodies of water—the Mediterranean functions as a warehouse for contaminants, so much so and with such few opportunities that the water is given to regenerate and purify itself through stronger currents, that the presence of contamination can become visually observable from the beach. Thus, this comment is made regarding the contaminants along the coast:

> "At the present, sewage is almost certainly the most significant pollutant of the Spanish coasts, both in the perception of the visitors and, in reality, as a threat to health. Sewage in sea water is a threat to the interests of the tourist industry for three reasons:"[154]

The reasons are thus enumerated: "...first it is possible that tourists may become ill through contact with sewage-contaminated sea water and thus a poor image of the Spanish coast could be created."[155]

The following reasons are also given: "...second, the aesthetic quality of the water is visibly reduced by sewage; and the third, seafood may be contaminated, and particularly if eaten raw may spread disease, again creating a bad image for the coasts. Tourists, influenced by media reporting of the polluted Mediterranean have become increasingly sensitive to all three factors."[156]

Although it has not been proven with certainty that cholera and typhoid fever can be contracted by swimming in water, which is slightly contaminated, it has been proven that eye, nose and ear infections are caused more frequently among swimmers who dip into waters in these conditions, as opposed to those who do not take the plunge. However, it has been found that it is not necessary to go into the water to suffer the effects of pollutants. Simply sitting on the beach can cause rashes to erupt

---

[154] SJ Kirby, "Recreation and Quality of Spanish Coastal Waters," in *Tourism in Spain: Critical Issues*, eds. Barke et al. (Wallingford: CAB International, 1996), 192
[155] Ibid. pp. 192.
[156] *Ibid.* pp. 192.

on the skin. In summary, it can be said that those who remain at a distance from the beaches and its waters remain in a better state of health than those who enjoy the so called "pleasures" of the sea and sand.

The largest contributor to this health problem is caused by the sewage water dumping into the sea. Up until the beginning of the decade of the 50's, this practice did not present a problem, as during the Franco regime, septic tanks were used systematically and was the preferred method of sewage disposal.

Later, with the avalanche of arriving tourists to the Costa del Sol, and its consequential development, the Ministry of Public Works found sufficient cause to authorize deep dumping in the sea or the treatment of sewage through filtering. These methods resulted to be costly and complex, and they were unable to keep up with the speed and rhythm of the area's tourism development.

This deplorable situation has been resolved to a great degree with the management of waters by the aforementioned public company, ACOSOL S.A. Long profundity wastewater discharges were installed at a distance of one kilometer from the beach. These have been both advisable and effective as this methodology has a positive historical trajectory.

In the decade of the 1940's, in, Los Angeles, it was proven that their effectiveness was a function of their scale. For a population of 10,000 inhabitants it is cheaper to construct a filtering plant. However, for a city of one million inhabitants it is more profitable to deal with sewage water through long profundity piping.

A second advantage is that such unattractive aesthetic effects of the contaminants are no longer visible to the tourists. Also, ecologically, the theory exists that residual waters are great carriers of nutrients in a maritime medium, which at present, lacks such elements. This nutritionally benefits the aquatic sea life, as well as the fishing industry of the region.

However, before releasing this sewage into the water, it has been proven, and in fact presently, is advisable to filter the water through numerous, already existing filters, as well as others, still in a state of planning, in order to increase their capacity for the future. In this way, the solid wastes are filtered from the residual waters, and they are released into the sea with a greater degree of security, as to their purity. (Graphs VII and VIII).

Legally, as a member of the European Union (EU), Spain must follow, and comply with the norms that regulate the quality of waters and beaches for bathing. The Ministry of Health and Consumer Affairs has the responsibility of informing the Union regarding this state of affairs. In order to keep current with the regulations of this governing body, the waters must be tested biweekly. In the past, the Atlantic beaches were in better microbiological conditions than Western Andalucía. These have shown improvement, however, in recent history.

The EU's system of aquatic quality is quite elemental in that it has a simple grading system of "pass" or "fail." On the other hand, Andalucía, on their own accord, has devised a more complete and complex method of control:

"Therefore, the Junta of Andalucía classifies beaches in greater detail, using the norms established by the Royal Decree 734/88. These norms are based on

EU reporting system. Five classes of water are assessed on a star rating system."[157]

Bishop continues: "Five stars indicate high ecological quality, four stars very good hygienic quality, three stars good hygienic quality, two stars 'regular' poor hygienic quality and one-star bad hygienic quality."[158]

In addition: "In addition to water quality, each beach is rated for hygienic/sanitary equipment (toilets with adequate sewage disposal, showers, drinking water, and changing facilities."[159]

Grades are awarded as well: "Grade 3 in the equipment category is awarded for sufficient equipment, grade 2 for insufficient equipment, grade 1 for inadequate equipment and grade 0 for complete absence of these facilities..."[160]

The classifications continue: "A third classification is based on the presence of a daily beach-cleaning program. Equipment and beach cleaning are not measures of water quality, but both can directly affect health hazards, so that local authorities are able to improve actual and perceived health conditions on beaches."[161]

And, finally, the author writes: "Standardized sights on outfalls are clearly indicated. The total length of the beaches covered by 1993 Andalucía Junta report is more than 574 km., more than 83% of the Andalusian coast."[162]

Also, the European Blue Flag plan exists for the protection of beaches and waters, which was launched in 1991. This program has become stricter and more extensive than the previous ones, as it also includes the marinas, which must satisfy 15 criteria, of quality.

The publicity given to these marinas and beaches, if they maintain the standards of cleanliness, is a great economic incentive for their tourism industry. The status of these destinations is maintained as public knowledge to the tourists at large. In this sense, and in general, Spanish beaches are among the cleanest of the continent. Although, it must be noted that the beaches of the Baleares Islands even surpass the quality of cleanliness of those of Andalucía.

The majority of the pollutants, which are found in the Costa del Sol, are generated by the same individuals who complain so much about them, that is to say, the tourists. It is of an organic type. It is public knowledge that if fish and the shellfish, are inadequately cooked, upon ingesting them, they can spread typhoid fever. Oysters, mussels and clams are the biggest culprits as carriers of this illness.

However, contaminants can come from industrial sources, as well. The effects of these are much more complex and far more unknown given their synergism. Now copper and zinc are found in the Tinto River. Mercury is found in the Mediterranean itself. The contamination also originates in the cement factories, which are located

---

[157] Paul L. Bishop, *Marine Pollution and Control*, (London: McGraw Hill, 1983), 200-201.

[158] *Ibid.* pp. 201-201.

[159] *Ibid.* pp. 200-201.

[160] *Ibid.* 200-201.

[161] Ibid. 200-201

[162] *Ibid.* 200-201

along the coastline. Pesticides used on agriculture, an activity, which has become modernized and intensified, represents a contaminant, as well.

Oil could fall within the category of an industrial pollutant, and given its recent history, this compound deserves special mention. The beaches of the Costa del Sol are littered with little black balls of tar. Though these are not unhealthful, this waste does detract from the beauty of the beaches. These are a product of the oil tanker traffic that anchor in Málaga, as well as in Cádiz, to unload their cargo of black gold en route to the refineries of Algeciras and Huelva.

Though very fortunately, this has not occurred up until the present, there is always the possibility that a tragedy could occur of the type, or of a similar magnitude to that, which occurred, in 1978, in Bretagne, France, with the Amoco, Cadiz. Such an occurrence would be disastrous for the Costa del Sol destination, as it would completely jeopardize all the tourism infrastructure.

The Provincial Board of Tourism of the Costa del Sol decides the rules and regulations, which include the municipalities which extend from Nerja to the east and towards Manilva in the west. This institution directly oversees the functioning of the golf courses. It, also receives funding from the Council of Andalucía. This has been crucial in the quality of the form and function of the beaches and boardwalks. This council has also been responsible for the construction of novelty structures, with the intent of giving what has been termed Spain's "crumbling coast" a facelift.

Regarding the improvement of beaches, the Board of Tourism, in the decade of the 90's, has fomented the relocation of 1,200,000 cubic meters of sand to the beaches of Fuengirola, and ever since has been watchful of the quantity of sand available to them. Málaga, in its campaign to promote itself as a tourist destination, has extended its beaches to Malagueta, at this time transferring a quantity of over 1,700,000 cubic meters of sand to it. The whole coast benefited from the added 7.2 million cubic meters of added sand (Barke M., France L. 1996)

At the beginning of the year 2000, construction began on the boardwalks of nine municipalities. Torremolinos and Carihuela, as well as that of Torre del Mar in Málaga, are being worked on, as they are found in much deteriorated conditions. The boardwalks of Nerja, Fuengirola and Marbella are also under construction.

In conclusion, it can be said that with the entrance of Spain in the EU, as well as Council of Andalucía's own regulations, along with the Tourism Board of the Costa del Sol, steps are being taken to improve the water of the Mediterranean, as well as its beaches. These measures are being accomplished in order to salvage the deteriorated image of the Costa del Sol in the eyes of both national, as well as international, tourism. This action comes as an acknowledgement of the fact that the tourism industry is very vulnerable and competitive, especially in the Mediterranean. Its fortune, or lack thereof, is a consequence capricious appeal at all levels. Golfers, however, seem to have carved out a more permanent presence among ever the changing trends of tourism along the Costa del Sol.

CHAPTER 8

The Life Cycle Theory of a Tourism Area and Cultural Geography of the Costa del Sol

This chapter makes an analysis of human settlements and urban developments along the western Costa del Sol. In other words, it is an approach to the area's cultural geography.

MÁLAGA AS A TOURIST DESTINATION

Málaga must be analyzed first and foremost, as the capital of the province, and as the largest city along the immediate coast. Historically, it played the role of a Phoenician port and, in the present, it is a principle port with ever increasing commercial activity. As was discussed in the previous chapter, oil is shipped to and received in Málaga (located near the mouth of the Guadalhorce River) for later distribution, throughout the rest of the nation.

The city of Malága's population is presently a little over half a million inhabitants. Since the end of the 19th century, and until the decade of the 50's, this province represented a tourist destination for national and international visitors alike. Among the international tourists, the main protagonists in this group were the British. In this sense, it is important to pay special attention to both the westerly, as well as eastern, population flows.

The proximity of Málaga to the British colony of Gibraltar, in the west made it historically a prime tourist destination for these nationals who arrive by land. During the Franco regime, the relationship between the dictatorship and this British settlement became icy, and a freeze was perceived by tourists, who arrived to the region. Visitors such as Laurie Lee and Sir Peter Chambers ("Sopita") could no longer be found along Málaga's coastline.

Also, at the beginning of the 50's, Málaga began to convert its luxury hotels—historically, for the use of tourism—into sanitariums or orphanages. This occurred as it lost its beaches and boardwalks to pollutants, which were a product of the commercial turn its economy took.

In the last decade, the Tourism Board of the Costa del Sol has tried to reinvent the image of the provincial capital, converting it, once again, into a tourism destination. This organization is making improvements on La Caleta, El Palo and Pedregadejo beaches, which are located on Malaga's eastern flank. Málaga truly always maintained a kind of reputation as a tourist destination among the Spaniards, above all, because of these beaches. Now, its reputation is increasing due to the improvement made on the beaches and the renewed construction of luxury four and five-star hotels.

The city is also being promoted as a destination for day trips. A bus trip is advertised that tours La Alcazaba, the Cathedral, the Gibralfaro Castile, the Picasso

Museum, the Bull Fighting Ring of Malagueta, the Roman theater, Town Hall, Malagueta Beach, La Victoria Sanctuary, the British Cemetery, the Flower Market and the Botanical Gardens. Also, flamenco shows are advertised periodically in various theaters. However, the personality of Málaga's tourism is to keep within a close perimeter of one's hotel, beach or golf course. This behavior has not been altered with much success.

Upon advancing in an analysis of the situation of the place, it could be concluded that Málaga is at a stage of stagnation or "pre-stagnation," in terms of its character as a tourist destination. It can be compared to numerous destinations in Florida, where because of their commercial nature, as well as their aging population, they are in stagnation. Tourism is no longer the main industry of these municipalities. Hotels have been converted into cheap apartments or retirement homes.

It remains to be seen if this policy of rejuvenation, undertaken by the municipality can save Málaga's reputation as a tourist destination. Butler maintains that a change in a tourist destination can only be successful and effective, if there is also a change in the function of the destination. A prime example of this is the previously discussed case of Atlantic City. This city introduced legal gambling in the beach hotels, which purposefully extended the tourist season. A qualitative and quantitative improvement took place, which was due to the functional variability of the location, thus proving Butler's premise.

THE SUB-REGION OF CHURRIANA

The tour operators sought out the location of the airport in Málaga, in order to spend less time on the transfer of tourists. The first of these destinations to the west of Málaga is Churriana. However, not until the late 90's did this town develop as a tourist destination, mainly because it lacked a beach. By the same token, its proximity to the airport ironically worked against it, as all its activity became a source of contaminants and noise. For reasons of security, doubts also grew regarding the soundness of the idea of locating tourist so close to the airport. In the 60's, this facility was also used as a military base.

However, as previously noted, Churriana has joined Málaga's campaign as a "green" or "environmentally friendly" point of interest for tourism. This has occurred in accordance with the capital of the province, as the town follows within the legislative jurisdiction of the main municipality. Tourism brochures have been published promoting the gardens and the two historical houses of El Retiro and of La Cónsula, to this end.

THE SUBREGION OF TORREMOLINOS

The next location west of Málaga that showed promise for tourism exploitation was Torremolinos. This is agreed upon by both Pollard and Domínguez, as they write: "Present-day Torremolinos is the result of the coalescence of two separate settlements,

Torremolinos itself and La Caihuela. The former was the more prosperous with an agricultural economy based primarily on sugar." [163]

The writers continue:

> Some agricultural processing took place, including the milling of grain, a fact reflected in the *molinos* element of the town's name. In addition, some fishermen inhabited cottages on the old cliff face leading down from San Miguel to Bajondillo. [164]

These writers continue to describe this once picturesque area:

> By contrast, La Carihuela was, exclusively a fishing settlement. Its inhabitants' economic condition was extremely precarious, and housing conditions were commensurately poor. [165]

Then in contrast, they explain:

> Of the two settlements, Torremolinos was by far the larger, for 12.7 ha compared with 1.04 ha for La Carihuela from the total built area of 16.9 ha, the remaining 3.2 ha being made up from buildings dispersed throughout the municipality. [166]

Needless to say, tourism profoundly altered such a rustic and primitive image. The beginning of its development in this sense took place between World War I and the Spanish Civil War. What was basically found at this stage of development were two small hotels located near the main downtown area of Torremolinos, another in Montemar, and as was customary, the villas and large homes in the hills with views of the sea and destined for Málaga's moneyed residents. There was also a golf course at that time.

The hotel industry began with the purchase of the Santa Clara Castle in 1898 by a British military official who found himself obliged to rent it and thus began the first founding of a hotel establishment in Torremolinos. Later, Doña Carlotta de Alessandri, whose name still appears on random exits of the N-340 highway, converted her farm into a hotel in 1934. There, the British were her first guests. It was situated in the Montemar area (Map I). Following this, even the Marquis of Nájera made its purchase in 1948.

Clearly by this time, Torremolinos was associated with an aristocratic tourism. It maintained this position well into the decade of the 50's. Ironically, the birth of tourism in this village had nothing to do with its geographic proximity to the airport. However, this juncture enhanced it for later development as a visitors' destination.

---

[163] John Pollard et al., "Unconstrained Growth: The Development of a Spanish Resort," Geography 80, no. 34 (January 1995): 33-34.
[164] *Ibid*. pp. 33
[165] *Ibid*. pp. 34
[166] *Ibid*. pp. 34.

The tourist industry did not begin to take similar shape to what it is today, until the 50's or 60's. This was due the problems of isolation that Spain experienced during and after World War II. During this period, the industry did not take off rapidly. The first luxury five-star hotel, with all the attributes of modernity, built in Torremolinos, was the Pez Espada. (See Map III)

During this time, land speculation began and increased. Many developers were British, German and Swedish. The idea was to build along the sea coast or at least with a view of it. The intent was to construct near commercial areas, as well as those of entertainment. However, as the price of land increased, with continuing speculation, towers of apartment buildings began to be erected on the beach.

The tour operators, who had financial interests in these urban developments, offered cheaper and cheaper vacation packages, in order to keep them full and producing. Consequentially, Torremolino's urban space suffered a drastic change in its external appearance, becoming what has been well known as, a "cement-jungle." The lodging went from being one appropriate for aristocrats to that of cheap three-star hotels. Its market was characterized as having become, instead, fit for "Good Time Charlie."

Perhaps, the most outstanding example of what the tourist market of Torremolinos has become is its Playamar complex. This development was originally touted as a luxurious addition to the coastline. It had 26 towers of 16 stories each. There, 6,000 people were warehoused. It is even said that the Generalissimo himself had commented on the horrific over-development taking place in Torremolinos.

Though its building permit was later rescinded, the Supreme Court of Madrid ordered the demolition of seven of its towers. This was due to the complaint of a Spanish homeowner who said that the towers blocked his view of the sea. This is a scandalous situation as an international, as well as national wakeup call, with respect to the anarchical state of development of Torremolinos.

Also, here it can be determined that this location has entered the phase of stagnation or "pre-stagnation" of Butler's Tourism Area Life Cycle Theory. This can be said, as the destination has begun to introduce artificial attractions to the destination, such as "Aqualand," an aquatic park.

There is, also "Crocodile Park," which is advertised as being the home to 300 crocodiles, an African fort, a Massai village, and a nursery for infant crocodiles. Live demonstrations with crocodiles are offered, where the opportunity is available to, physically, touch them. This center also contains a mini-zoo, with other types of animals, an African store, swing sets, as well as a cafeteria, clearly offering a family atmosphere.

However, the existence of these parks, with artificial attractions, symbolizes that the area is entering into the stagnation phase according to the TALC. Its development has been so uncontrolled, irregular and incoherent that Torremolinos earned itself a poor reputation, both internationally and in Spain itself. Problems of crime and disorderly conduct have occurred and have been publicized in the media, which have served to dissuade tourists from visiting the destination.

In spite of these issues, rays of hope do exist for its rejuvenation. At present, the Council of Andalucía is sponsoring an intensive planting of shrubbery and trees in public parks and boardwalks. The intent is to renovate the urban center and restore the existing buildings. The intention is to keep traffic under control with urban strategies and measures and with the future development of six kilometers of boardwalk space.

THE SUB-REGION OF BENALMÁDENA

The next westerly town is Benalmádena, which in contrast to Torremolinos, has never been under the jurisdiction of the municipality of Málaga. However, what has occurred is that this space has taken on a similar aspect to that of Torremolinos. This spatial occurrence has been the result of Benalmádena, functioning as a receptacle, for the urban activity that could find no place in the former destination. Even though in the 70's, Benalmádena represented a center, which attracted a fairly high level of tourism. By the 80's, the same pattern of three-star hotels and inexpensive vacation package could be identified.

Spatially, in Benalmádena, the same system of urban sprawl is present as in Torremolinos. Towards its interior, the place follows in longitude, by making its axis the Málaga Cádiz road, the N-340, or otherwise known as the "Road of Death," as was discussed in another chapter of this book. As this highway also traverses Torremolinos, there is no real transition between the two urban centers. Given the spatial fusion of these towns, the only articulation of Benalmádena's existence is a sign announcing it, posted along the highway.

In Benalmádena: "However, as in Torremolinos, there is a considerable variety, within the municipal area itself, reflecting the operation of land speculation and ownership patterns at various phases of the area's development."[167]

These authors continue regarding the historical spatial development of this municipality: "In the mid-1950's to the mid-1960's such activity was concentrated on the flatter areas in the east of the municipio, with the fragmentation of some large units of ownership into smaller parcels for direct sale to future occupants of homes and villas."[168]

The citation continues:

> At the same time in the Benalmádena Coast area, a number of small land units, were being considered by a property developing company, with a view to developing a large *urbanización*. From the mid-1960's to the early 1970's actual development proceeded much more rapidly and was located more in the center and west of the municipal coastal area."[169]

This municipality was in contrast with Mijas and Marbella during this period, in that most of the property being developed for tourism was in the hands of Spaniards. Originally, these properties were farms, which gave Benalmádena a fragmented and

[167] M. Barke and L. France, "The Costa del Sol," in *Tourism in Spain: Critical Issues*, ed. M. Barke et al. (Wallingford: CAB International, 1996), 280.
[168] *Ibid.* pp. 280.
[169] *Ibid.* pp . 280

disperse quality to its spatial appearance. This type of residential tourism development tends to produce isolated housing units.

Arroyo de la Miel is worth mentioning, as it represented high density and low-cost housing, built for the satisfaction of the residential needs of construction workers and for the needs of workers involved in the tourist industry in general. This neighborhood finally became the downtown center of the municipality of Benalmádena. However, its ultimate transformation occurred when it became the choice place of residence for low-income and elderly British residents.

Benalmádena maintains a better stature, in terms of tourism, than Torremolinos, in spite of a fraudulent scandal, which occurred in the 70's regarding the Torrequebrada development. Insult was literally added to injury when eight floors of the luxury hotel El Riviera partially collapsed.

However, its superior image in comparison with neighboring Torremolinos, is due in part to its charming downtown, which conserves the appearance of an authentic Andalusian village. Benalmádena's healthy participation in the western Costa del Sol's tourism activity is confirmed with the addition of its port, from where the Dolphin's Tourism excursion departs, as well as fishing trips. This thriving center is also home to the Tivoli World amusement park and the Torrequebrada Casino.

THE SUB-REGION OF FUENGIROLA

Following the western direction, Fuengirola is found. Three-star hotels, as well as massified tourism are also found here, as well as in Torremolinos and Benalmádena. The difference, between the former and the later destinations, is rooted in the sociological component of the industry, as in Fuengirola, the population which predominates are visitors in family units. Notably, the properties which can be acquired here are those of the small house type, apartments or time-shares.

Fuengirola's main attraction is its zoo. Its tourist brochure advertised that neither cages nor bars will be found on its premises. It is touted as being a genuine reproduction of a tropical forest. The visitor is encouraged to enjoy the experience of taking a stroll through a jungle, without missing even the smallest detail. The brochure goes on to say, "Visit the tropical forests of Madagascar, Southeast Asia and Equatorial Africa." According to the zoo, native animals from each of these ecosystems are to be found there, along with their life-styles represented in their primary state.

According to the publicity made available by the zoo, in the waters of Manglar, it can be seen from a close vantage point how large tortoises and colored fish live side by side. This is a prize-winning recreation, internationally recognized by the XXII Edition of the Annual Conference of the European Association of Zoos and Aquaria in September of 2005. In this type of tourism supply, there is a clear ecological slant. The area refers to itself as a zoo in constant evolution. Here, there is no better thing to do than to enjoy nature in the exuberance of a tropical forest and, at the same time, fight for its conservation.

It is said that the park participates in no less than 35 species reproduction programs that are in danger of extinction. Its activities are directed, in this space, to conservation of the virgin areas of the planet. Finally, the park promotes itself by saying that, in this pioneering Spanish exhibition, aviary life, as well as mammals may be enjoyed, as observed in this idyllic environment. If a tourist wants to plan his or her calendar for a visit, the park promoters, advise that mother nature never sleeps, and during the months of July and August, a tour unique to all of Europe, through the leafy forests of Africa and Asia, can be enjoyed. To top the visit off, a delicious dinner may be enjoyed in the heart of the forest.

THE SUB-REGION OF MIJAS

A pause must be made at the municipality of Mijas, which is located between Marbella and Fuengirola. This space is divided into two areas: Mijas Coast and Mijas Village. Historically, this site was known for its agricultural settlements, which gradually became tourist settlements. The largest golf course in Spain, as it was confirmed to be in January 2007, is located here. This is the most outstanding feature of the municipality. This golf course, the already mentioned La Cala, stands in what previously was a farm and is formed by three courses: the Asia Course, the America Course and the Andalucía Course.

This extensive property also includes a five-star hotel and a spa. There are various types of housing developments featuring different type of homes, which supposedly were built with the greatest respect for the natural environment and the ecological movement of the times. Housing has been designed following basically three formats. Luxury apartments are available, townhouses, or the most expensive, semi-attached villas, which can cost as much as one million euros (La Cala Resort Newsletter, 2007).

A significant fact—and at the same time, a symbolic one—is that this property complex is owned by a group of Irish investors. This puts Mijas in second place along the Costa del Sol, as a recipient of foreign investment. The first place goes to Marbella, the case of which will be examined in the following section. Although, the residents are of different nationalities, the place clearly has a British or Irish feel, as the players or guests here belong predominantly to these nationalities. A standardization and "placelessness" are perceived at the property, as well as a situation of isolation, regarding the Andalusian space. The menus of the restaurants are designed with taste buds of the customers in mind, and there is even a golf competition organized, prized with a trophy, in honor of the celebration of St. Patrick's Day.

Perhaps, the ingredient of greatest importance to the totality of the Spanish nation is its high-speed train, AVE, which joins Madrid to Málaga. La Cala has the expectations that this railway will bring more golfers to its doors in a shorter time and in a greater quantity, as the trip, from start to finish, only takes two hours. This service is thought to benefit La Cala as:

"There now over 83,000 licensed golfers in the Madrid area, an increase of 8.5% over 2005. La Cala's commercial director, says the oversupply of players in the Madrid region offers a great opportunity for the resort. 'Being the biggest golf resort in Spain, we have the facilities to welcome and accommodate large numbers of golfers."[170]

The commercial director of the La Cala resort continues to state:

"To date, most of our Spanish visitors come in the summer months, during their annual vacations. With the imminent opening of the high-speed AVE link and given our fantastic weather, we are now preparing to receive more Madrid golfers from the area."[171]

This optimism may have a basis. However, if Strapp's theory is recalled, in his study of Sauble Beach, this scientist reaches a different conclusion. He draws upon Butler's Tourism Area Life Cycle theory, in which it is premised by its author that the prolonged extension of a tourism stage is healthier for a destination than one of short stays. Applying this theory, Strapp himself notes that the possibility due to easy access, allowing for the capability of only one-day stays to the vacation space, places the case of study in the stagnation phase of the theory.

In this way, it could result that, upon spending such a short time at the destination, the tourists never acquire a full feeling of belonging to the destination. To this end, the jury is still out as to how short-stay tourism will affect the Andalusian space.

THE SUB-REGION OF MARBELLA

Continuing westward, and in contrast with the previously mentioned municipalities, Marbella is to be found. Its character performs as a magnet attracting visitors and residents of a higher social and economic category. Here, the norm has been to favor foreign investors, in comparison with the rest of the Costa del Sol and Spain, in general, though certain Spaniards have participated with their investment in the development of the area.

The first of these representatives was Ricardo Soriano, or the Marquis of Ivanrey, who purchased land in this location, when it was only an unknown village. Soriano decided upon this transaction, in order to practice his favorite past time, fishing, with more ease and comfort. Up until then, he had practiced this sport in the, comparably at the time, overdeveloped French tourist destination of Biarritz.

The exclusive Marbella Club opened its doors in 1954. Its first founder and owner was Prince Hohenlohe, nephew of the Marquis of Ivanrey. This club featured a bar and restaurant, as well as a hotel for the European and Spanish elite. The establishment became known as the most aristocratic meeting place along the Costa del Sol.

It served such well-known clients, aside from the Hohenlohe, as the Duke and Earl of Windsor, the Generalissimo's daughter, and Princess Alexandra and Angus

---

[170] La Cala Resort Newsletter, Summer 2007, (3).
[171] Ibid. pp. 3

Ogilvy, who spent their honeymoon there. American celebrities, such as Frank Sinatra, as well as many more recent, movie stars, and politicians were also welcomed at this locale. This tourism center continues to command prestige and distinction in the area, in spite of the fact that it was purchased in the 80's by a group of Arab investors.

Another protagonist, in the development of Marbella, was José Banús, the Spanish development king of this era. He was the creator of Puerto Banús, the most luxurious marina on the Costa del Sol, which is located to the west of downtown Marbella. It is typical to find impressive yachts, belonging to worldwide jetsetters, anchored there. It is also the favorite place of boating recreation for the sheiks of oil exporting countries.

During the 1980's, the Costa del Sol's general reputation, as has been discussed earlier, began to decline. The so-called "Coast of Concrete," also came to be known as the "Coast of Crime." This occurred as drug traffickers and the European Mafia began to find their niche in the region. Within this negative picture, which was being painted for the tourist industry, as even street robberies were reported and began to escalate, the figure of Jesús Gil arose from the calamity.

Jesús Gil was a constructor, and also held the prestigious position of president of the soccer team, the Atlético de Madrid. Gil was elected mayor of Marbella in 1991. It was well known in the community, and the whole country, for that matter, that he had only accepted this political position in order to perform a massive cleanup of a community that was in drastic deterioration. Gil had an axe to grind in improving the quality of Marbella's society. He owned two apartment buildings that he was unable to sell because of the reputation the municipality had acquired. To this end, it was said that his tactics were sometimes questionable.

However, currently, though blue-collar crime has all but disappeared, Marbella's corrupt authorities have allowed the sinuous path of white collar crime, involving money laundering, embezzlement and bribery to continue. One of these nightmares for the Marbella population, was called "Operation Malaya." Its head was personified in Juan Antonio Roca, whose prominence in the Marbella municipal administration goes back to the days of Luis Gil. During that time, he was the Municipal Urban Area Assessor and the Urban Manager of the Municipality.

Roca was just one of a long laundry list of administrators who were accused of controlling Marbella's citizen's taxes and having invested them in luxury cars, expensive real estate in Madrid, works of art, as well as designer clothing. This scandal exploded in March of 2005, and it still is causing repercussions.

This police operation opened the way for an uninterrupted succession of police investigations regarding other possible cases of urban corruption in Spain. Another one of its tentacles was discovered to be the so-called "Operation White Whale." This was case of urban corruption in the Costa del Sol was unraveled and solved through telephone tapping on the part of the authorities.

The light at the end of this tunnel, in which the citizens of Marbella seem to have grown accustomed to being horrified, has been the efficient functioning of the Anti-Corruption District Attorney's Office and the police. These agencies work tirelessly and honestly to remove, as much as possible, the cancerous tumor that began to grow in the 1990's. This diseased, yet perfect symbiosis, between construction, and politics found fertile ground to grow and thrive in an atmosphere distinguished by conviviality and negligence of political parties and police.

In spite of Marbella's predominantly elitist personality, social and economic diversity could be located in San Pedro de Alcántara, a town near Marbella. This surprisingly socioeconomically differentiated area, found in such a small geographical space, is a function of the necessary lodging for construction workers and in general tourism industry workers. These workers are not confined only to Spanish nationals. Currently they come from North Africa or other European countries, such as Romania, and even the Far East. These sectors make up two thirds of the active population (Marchana Gómez 1988).

THE SUB-REGION OF ESTEPONA

Closer to the British possession of Gibraltar than Málaga's airport, Estepona is found. Historically, as a tourist destination, it catered more to the national market. Only recently has it found its bearings at the level of the international industry. It has accomplished this by marketing its land for the consumption of residential tourism. This commercial facet is a now a major player in the Spanish tourism panorama.

This product has experienced a true economic takeoff since the establishment of social, economic and political relations between the Spanish Nation and Gibraltar. Previous to this new diplomatic agreement, during the Franco regime, with the closing of the border of Gibraltar, Estepona was isolated and distanced with respect to international tourism. This center was much more removed from this industry than all the rest of the urban areas along the Costa del Sol.

Therefore, the scarcity of hotel beds in the space is of relatively little importance, in comparison with the astounding growth of housing developments. These developments began blanketing Estepona's coast in the 1980's. It is expected that this phenomenal development will not take on that of Mijas. More regulations have been put in place regarding coastal urban planning, than there were a decade ago. However, in Gibraltar, the real estate agencies advertise beautiful houses for sale along the coast of Estepona. This represents a very wise investment for the British pocketbook, given the exchange-rate between the euro and the generally powerful sterling pound.

Currently, Spain is targeting this type of residential tourism as it contributes more to the national coffers than the cheap tourism of three-star hotels. However, these structures place more pressure on and are more of a burden on the environment.

In this way:

> "The model of housing developments, with crystal clear swimming pools are, implicitly and explicitly, water wasteful...The Costa del Sol is an insatiable glutton of this resource. The main reason is that, not only is water

a resource of prime necessity, but it is also an ingredient that represent a social status, as the garden, the pool and the golf course are flaunted."[172]

The author continues in his protest:

"This status is measured in square meters of green space and it comes with a sacrifice of water. A symptom of this is that the average consumption per inhabitant is 400 liters per day. This stands way above the national average. This diagnosis is made by Javier de Luis, Coordinator of Ecologists in Action in Marbella."[173]

This quotation is applicable to Estepona, as well as to any municipality, that is located on Spain's dry coast, and that targets and develops residential tourism.

FINAL CONSIDERATIONS

Finally, and in conclusion, it can be said that Richard W. Butler's Tourism Area Life Cycle can be applied to the Costa del Sol. It is a mature area that has cycled through the various stages of growth of a tourism destination. According to Butler, these phases are those of exploration, participation, development, consolidation and stagnation. This last stage may lead to either the phase of decline or rejuvenation.

The Costa del Sol may be considered a macro-region, both geographically and economically, as it primarily is dedicated to the activity of tourism. At the same time, it is composed of municipal sub-regions, which also dedicate their productive efforts to this same industry. The largest of these is the provincial capital of Málaga. This city is trying to exit the stagnation phase, along with its neighbor Churriana. This city is a judicial dependent of Málaga, and both are making efforts to present a form of ecological tourism and one-day stays.

Towards the west, the other sub-regions are found. They too are all located in the stagnation or "pre-stagnation" phase, as designated in this study. This can be said as both private and public sectors have tried to introduce artificial features, along with the accompanying infrastructure, in these areas. Golf courses, among them the La Cala Golf Course in Mijas, which is the biggest in all of Spain.

In terms of these sports installations (Torremolinos is the only urban center which does not respond to the demand for this activity, and, therefore, does not showcase a golf course), even though these areas contribute to the national and regional coffers, they waste the very scarce and precious resource of this Dry Spain, water. In fact, in order to resolve the conflictive situation of the necessities of water consumption of the population and those of the courses, water filters have been installed along coast, and more are to be installed in the future. (Graphs III and IV). Technology, and not mother nature, may be the only buffers for a thirsty coastline and its sub-regions, with diametrically opposing priorities regarding water consumption.

---

[172] José Bejarano, "El monstruo insaciable de la Costa del Sol," *La Vanguardia*, (August 2, 2005)
[173] *Ibid.*

CHAPTER 9

Conclusions

New Findings and Conclusions

The most novel conclusions of this study are two-fold. First and foremost a new stage has been added to the Tourism Area Life Cycle Theory, which, within this context, has been given the name of the "Pre-Stagnation" stage.

The introduction of a new cycle to the already established stages is allowed and found to be appropriate, in general, as well as specifically in the stage of the Costa del Sol. In this way, it can be said that a tourism destination may have a well-established image, and yet, differing from the classical TALC theory, is still fashionable and functional.

These characteristics, however, do not imply that the tourist area does not experience problems similar to those of a space in stagnation, which include problems of a sociological, environmental, as well as economic nature. Also, this same tourist destination may offer imported attractions to its tourists, another characteristic of the stagnation stage.

Thus, for the first time, a new stage in the TALC has been created and applied to the Costa del Sol, in particular. It is an ideal conceptualization for this destination. However, it can be extrapolated to any tourism space, which presents a paradoxical situation of having a mature image, yet is still feasibly fashionable.

This newly created phase of "Pre-Stagnation," also combines characteristics of the classical stagnation phase of the TALC. As the destination must offer imported tourist attractions in order to fully meet the requirements of this phase. The Costa del Sol is a perfect example of this. As has been underlined throughout this book, this coast has, both extensively and intensively, imported golf courses to the area, which are artificial elements to its natural environment. As has been reiterated, they are monetarily profitable, yet they are a cause of ecological concern.

Subjective and Objective Aspects of the Golf Courses

Although golf courses are put into play, relatively less than the crowded beaches, overflowing with tourists, enjoying the sea, sun and sand, their environmental impact is far greater. With these, spatial land patterns and holdings, along with their native flora and fauna, are altered. The pesticides used in order to maintain their vegetation have an impact on the ecosystem, which still have not yet been fully studied or understood.

That is why it can be affirmed, without a doubt, that although its numerical exploitation by tourists is less, the environmental damage these courses cause is far greater. This can be stated without arriving at the main fact of their astounding consumption of water, which depletes the population's drinking water resources, if recycled water is not used for their irrigation.

In the Costa del Sol, it can be argued that under the present conditions of the consumption of water golf courses use, they are, both subjectively and objectively, an unsustainable tourist attraction. This theory has an objective basis, however. Just in Marbella, there are, in existence, 33 square kilometers of golf courses. In the high season, which is in the months from May to September, they consume 10 liters of water per day per square meter of vegetation.

Until very recently, and still to a certain degree, even the usage of recycled water had been rejected for the irrigation of these spaces. The owners of these tourist attractions sustained that this type of processed water damages the grass, due to its high sodium and nitrate content. They maintained that the odor was bothersome to the golfers, as well. Therefore, the specialists of the Association of Andalucía have discovered 350 wells of drinking water functioning, in these housing developments. The Environmental Council, in July of 2005, opened 58 legal proceedings for the illegal collection of water.

This unsustainable situation of the consumption of this resource by the courses can also be approached subjectively. A judgment may be formulated as to the change this impact has caused on the environment. This transformation may be measured, in terms of the difference between the reality of the modification of the surroundings, and the negative opinions the people and their governing bodies have regarding this situation.

The solution to the major damage depends on the objectives of the public administration, the judgment of the experts on the subject and the priorities of the public opinion in general. It is to be remembered that for some experts the carrying capacity is the level beyond the point where impacts exceed specified levels of given standards of evaluation. The majority of conflicts of opinion regarding the carrying capacity of a tourism destination exist because of these standards. That is to say, the differences arise because of subjective opinions and not due to the availability of resources.

In the case of the Costa del Sol, both the subjective, as well as objective, evaluation aspects are fused, given the present consumption of the golf course's water consumption. These, also, are extensive to the golf courses not yet built, as this insatiable rhythm cannot continue. In terms of the coast, the impressive growth of the urban coast is terminating with the existence of the habitat of its coastal ecosystems. In terms of the land, or inward sea, the pressure of human activity is annihilating what was left of the water systems, the wetlands and the beach dunes, the forests and scrubland. Erosion of the land also continues, and the aquifers are becoming salinized.

Consequentially, this space is an ideal area in which to experiment with the application of Butler's Tourism Area Life Cycle (TALC) theory. The seed of this concept first appeared in print, in 1972, in a joint paper presented by Richard W. Butler and Jim Brougham, entitled "The Applicability of the Asymptotic Curve to the Forecasting of Tourism Development." This was the inception of the mentioning of the "tourism area life cycle." Although, the purpose of this presentation was to study tourism flow, it was not until 1980 that Butler completely and extensively developed his theory in an article entitled, "The Concept Tourist Area Cycle of Evolution: Implications for Management of Resources."

THE CONCEPT OF A TOURISM DESTINATION CYCLE

It can be said that with this article, Butler did not make any ground-breaking discoveries. He merely joined the dots of a vital system that every person in existence understands, that is to say, the process of life and death, birth and decline. The novelty in Butler's discovery is that he applies it to a geographical space, which is dedicated to the activity of tourism.

It can even be said that knowingly, or unknowingly, Butler uses the contradictory forces of the Hegelian system of dialectics in his analysis. Through these, he proves that a tourism destination is as organically vital, as any other living organism. It can be as vulnerable to misfortune as any other being. In its vital journey, it has the capacity to fall into demise or regenerate.

In this study, the intent is to prove that the Costa del Sol is in the stagnation, yet more precisely, the "Pre-Stagnation" phase. This period of development, devised in this study, for this tourist destination, however, can also be applied to others, which display the same characteristics, such as the introduction to the destination of artificial attractions. That is to say, a mature destination which, in order to increase its demand, has found itself in the position of diversifying its tourism attractions. The tourism market is capricious and trendy and, therefore, this destination, or others like it have had to find alternatives to their traditional product of sea, sun and sand. These alternatives, in the case of the Costa del Sol, have taken on the form of golf courses. However, the possibility exists that the Costa del Sol may still fall into decline if it continues to consume, at the current rate, its precious and scarce resource of water.

TEMPORAL CONCLUSIONS REGARDING THE COSTA DEL SOL

These opposing forces may develop, both temporally and spatially. Butler's theory allows for the flexibility of applying it, both in the historical as well as geographical sense. It is, therefore, a crucial as well as determinative tool for conceptual study and analysis. In this study, the intent has been made to apply Sandra Corack's article entitled, "The Modification of the Tourism Area Life Cycle Model for (Re)Juvenating a Destination: The Case of the Opatija Riviera, Croatia." This scientist took the TALC's conceptual model and applied its stages of development to the history of this tourism area.

By the same token, it is understood that for the first time, said theoretical body has been taken and its tourism development has been applied to its phases, that is those of exploration, participation, development, consolidation and stagnation, and finally, that of "pre-stagnation," particularly created as well as designated here, and that of decline have been applied to the historical trajectory of the Costa del Sol.

The first tourists arriving at this space, who were mainly British "explorers", have been defined, as well as its interrupted stage of development, due to internal and external conflict, not to mention international political policy. The tourism boom, which took off in the 60's, is analyzed, which inaugurated cheap tourism of three-star hotels in places such as Torremolinos.

As has been reiterated, upon having analyzed the path of historical tourism in the Costa del Sol, this study sustains that this coast is in the stagnation, but primarily, the "pre-stagnation" phase. This situation could give way to its entrance into the phase of decline. This is happening, precisely, because of the type of tourism created by the sport of golf. These golfers contribute more financially to the Andalusian Association.

They are predominately males, with greater purchasing power, prolonged vacation time and, thus, these men are more predisposed to paying top-dollar for services during their vacation time. This can be confirmed upon making the comparison to the massive charter flights and three-star hotel tourism of the 70's.

However, though this sector of tourists, make more of a quantitative contribution to the economy of the Costa del Sol, it negatively impacts the area by taking away from its natural resources, that being primarily its source of water. This Spanish coast does not have the capacity within its aquifer resources to irrigate these greens. If the development of the industry is not supported by recycled water, there will be no more room for the prolongation of tourism and the Costa del Sol will fall into decline.

Butler offers the phase of rejuvenation as the last and alternate possibility to the former. However, the intent of this study is to unquestionably demonstrate that this phase will never be reached, if recycled water is not used along this Spanish coast. This procedure should be, intensively and extensively, accomplished by the public company, ACOSOL, already described and analyzed in another chapter of this book.

SPATIAL CONCLUSIONS REGARDING THE COSTA DEL SOL

Regarding the spatial application of the Tourism Area Life Cycle theory, parallelisms, however seemingly unlikely, have been drawn between the development of the Mediterranean destination, Venice, and that of the Costa del Sol, also a Mediterranean destination. This has been done by drawing between them the comparison that they are two mature tourist destinations. They differ from each other in that Venice is an historical city, and the Costa del Sol is a region. In spite of their differences, similarities in the settlements in their geographical spaces have been found.

In order to perform this analysis, Paolo Antonio Russo's article, "A Re-Foundation of the TALC for Heritage Cities" has been used. In this article the concept of "vicious cycle" has been created and defined for the case of Venice and, for the purpose of this study, the same concept has been applied to the Costa del Sol.

In the municipality of Venice, and in the multiple municipalities of the Costa del Sol, the "willingness to spend" is being lost and this leads to a loss of income and expenditures of revenue for these municipalities alike. When this stage has taken place, there has already been an economic, social and spatial reorganization of the space. Jointly, and overlapping this regionalization, what Russo terms, as the Functional Tourist Region (FTR) is created. Tourists and excursionists find cheaper lodging here than in the downtown center of Venice.

The difference in the Spanish case lies in the nature of the resources that are lost. Along the Costa del Sol, it is not so much revenue that is lost, but one of an ecological nature, that is to say, water. The unbridled and wasteful watering of golf courses with drinking water is bringing the population nuclei, along the coast, to its environmental knees.

This situation currently signifies a loss of resources and a dismantling of an entire ecological system. An extreme scenario could present itself as a complete paralysis of all tourism, including residential activity of the area. It is without a doubt, that the present situation represents stagnation, however, a phase of "pre-stagnation," more appropriately defined in this study, for this tourist space could conceivably conclude in its decline.

Upon performing a spatial analysis of the Costa del Sol, this type of tourist can be viewed as making its presence there. They are located in satellite nuclei of population, in artificial environments, separate from the coastal cities. Their developments consume, in their majority water captured from well water. These patterns may be terminated with the Decree on Golf Courses, which has been in redaction since 2004, by the Councils on the Environment, the Ministry of Public Works, and that of Tourism and Sports. Its principal precept is to separate golf courses from housing development, with the expressed prohibition of allowing them to construct more in the future.

In the different drafts of this legislation, exceptions are permitted, as long as the housing developments are of a reduced size. Also, they would have to be located at a minimum distance from the courses and, at the same time, containing a very small density of construction. If the edification of hotels is allowed, they too must be low density. To this point, only a maximum of three built floors is permitted, with 300 beds for an 18-hole course and 400 beds for a 27-hole course. Its most important stipulation is that recycled water must be used for its entire irrigation.

As has been reiterated, in this study, it has been maintained that the Costa del Sol finds itself in the stage of stagnation of Richard Butler's TALC theory or the "pre-stagnation" phase customized and conceptualized, in this book, for its application to this space. However, the latter phase of "pre-stagnation," product of this study can be validly applied, as well to other mature tourist destinations that are still fashionable and have introduced artificial tourism attractions.

Outside of the regional framework, there is, of course, the global dimension, which can also affect this Spanish coastal space. This magical people, whose veins carry Hebrew, Arab and European blood, can doubtless be affected by climate change.

THE ECOLOGICAL FUTURE OF THE COSTA DEL SOL

The existing phenomenon of climate change, already accepted by the scientific community, is invading its beaches. This Mediterranean Sea, whose name means "in the middle of land," could become such a threat that it absorbs the Spanish coastline, in general, especially the vulnerable coast dealt with in this book.

Though the consequences are not yet known with certainty, it can be affirmed that the melting of the polar ice caps, as well as the glaciers of Greenland, will cause sea levels to rise globally. In fact, Greenland's glaciers are melting at a rate two times more quickly than what had been expected, that is at about eight kilometers yearly. Although, it can only be speculated how this will affect the beaches, of the Costa del Sol, these being its major attraction.

According to NASA, and other organizations 2005, and all years successively after that, registered the hottest temperature ever recorded. The temperature for 2016 was 1.57 degrees Fahrenheit above the 20th century average of 58.6. Also, according to the interview maintained with Juan Cantos, director of the Río Real Monteros golf course, a phenomenon similar to the increase in water consumption is occurring. The director related that climate change in Europe is causing winters to be warmer, thus extending their golf season.

In this way, the price of greens fees is descending. Prior to climate change, the high season was precisely winter, when the icy and snowy weather of the northerly countries made the practice of golf impossible. The low season is June, July, and August. The hotter the weather, the less pleasant it is to play golf. If climate change continues, it will become more and more uncomfortable to practice during the summer months.

However, the phenomenon affecting Europe is more complex than this. The so-called Atlantic transmitting ribbon, or the Atlantic thermal line, runs the risk of no longer functioning. This marine current keeps the continent from freezing over in winter. If this were to happen, the temperatures of Greenland would descend, and this would have a disastrous effect on Europe.

Global climate change could be a threat to our society as we know it. This has been proven with the forest fires that have taken place in the western U.S. since 2007 and especially during 2017 and 2018. In these years, these fires were intensified in Southern California, another Mediterranean climate.

The efforts made in the Costa del Sol to regulate the situation of the golf courses and reduce the vulnerability of the aquatic resources may prove to be impossible. Then too, theories such as that of the Tourism Area Life Cycle, implemented at the community or tourism destination level, will become useless and irrelevant. The irony is found in the paradox of the reality that the creating force of all the wealth that stimulated and produced the growth of tourism, that is to say, the industrial revolution could be the cause of its demise.

However, an analysis of this phenomenon would be at another level and the subject of another book, yet to be explored...

Appendices

CHARTS AND GRAPHS
COURTESY OF ACOSOL S.A.
PEDRO MUNOZ LUQUE
CHIEF OF COMPREHENSIVE SANITATION PLANNING
2018

CHART I: VOLUME IN RESERVOIRS Hm^3

MONTH YEAR	JANUARY	FEBRUARY	MARCH	APRIL	MAY	JUNE	JULY	AUGUST	SEPTEMBER	OCTOBER	NOVEMBER	DECEMBER	ANNUAL AVERAGE
1989	38,310	58,719	59,299	58,947	56,667	52,260	45,942	39,458	34,686	36,757	52,089	51,729	48,739
1990	54,765	56,253	61,433	61,475	61,122	57,048	52,013	45,265	39,543	34,908	34,819	39,441	49,907
1991	38,564	46,264	59,941	60,604	58,408	54,081	47,934	40,707	34,790	36,977	34,775	37,264	45,859
1992	35,617	40,370	42,581	46,207	42,497	39,796	34,729	28,160	22,898	20,742	17,907	15,782	32,257
1993	14,135	21,214	25,103	24,656	25,065	22,456	18,567	14,004	10,781	9,794	30,336	31,563	20,640
1994	33,132	33,649	34,936	33,428	30,896	26,510	20,764	14,388	9,772	7,650	7,260	5,007	21,533
1995	5,528	5,149	4,414	3,458	2,593	1,568	0,882	0,500	0,472	0,528	1,139	21,962	4,016
1996	55,182	58,826	60,153	60,679	61,430	60,953	57,646	53,399	50,075	48,760	50,287	54,063	56,020
1997	54,195	59,584	60,932	60,574	59,352	57,351	53,019	48,219	46,549	46,587	52,924	52,943	54,352
1998	56,024	55,055	59,100	59,015	58,810	55,961	51,710	46,682	43,037	39,847	37,148	36,150	49,853
1999	37,399	37,601	41,653	42,784	42,733	40,100	34,966	29,222	25,078	27,623	27,053	28,288	34,608
2000	44,320	49,528	49,699	56,993	59,963	58,678	54,689	49,737	44,792	41,248	39,965	56,020	50,469
2001	57,141	56,804	57,309	57,751	56,003	51,881	45,695	38,935	34,493	32,668	38,412	56,467	48,632
2002	57,794	58,468	60,237	61,702	60,279	56,445	50,571	43,071	37,834	33,857	36,786	49,205	50,496
2003	58,025	59,816	61,340	60,764	60,427	56,635	50,249	42,328	35,913	43,763	56,004	53,626	53,308
2004	55,982	56,350	57,208	59,500	59,142	55,814	48,680	42,902	37,196	33,620	30,173	31,416	47,339
2005	28,672	26,357	35,069	34,759	31,208	25,986	19,259	12,227	7,155	5,409	5,556	6,922	19,948
2006	16,213	28,208	51,539	57,309	57,267	54,651	49,600	43,543	38,051	36,600	52,051	54,347	45,029
2007	55,413	58,341	58,131	58,764	57,141	52,488	46,701	40,539	36,682	34,729	32,984	42,058	47,833
2008	48,339	53,968	57,583	60,363	59,247	55,392	49,471	42,682	40,539	40,994	52,507	54,803	51,328
2009	54,460	57,246	58,173	57,141	53,911	49,376	43,560	36,771	31,623	27,968	25,423	54,908	45,882
2010	54,727	56,382	61,684	61,648	61,467	57,941	51,843	44,708	39,593	35,528	34,360	54,045	51,227
2011	54,158	57,120	62,276	60,932	61,900	59,837	54,844	49,110	44,283	42,020	53,600	53,531	54,480
2012	52,621	50,951	48,560	46,321	44,202	39,830	34,138	27,904	24,855	26,063	55,098	54,992	42,128
2013	56,698	56,656	58,341	62,014	61,594	58,994	53,455	47,403	42,750	39,087	35,454	33,368	50,485
2014	32,698	39,711	39,357	40,657	34,429	34,729	28,467	22,082	18,775	17,542	33,475	43,577	32,163
2015	47,744	50,306	58,046	59,015	56,382	52,280	46,094	39,982	35,617	35,218	39,104	37,720	46,459
2016	36,994	37,753	37,720	39,441	57,983	55,708	50,700	43,948	38,209	34,789	40,404	54,708	44,036
2017	55,308	57,077	59,605	59,774	58,763	54,651	49,395	43,948	37,956	34,729	33,102	31,771	48,007

VOLUME IN RESERVOIRS Hm^3

CHART II: FUTURE STATE OF RECYCLING NETWORKS

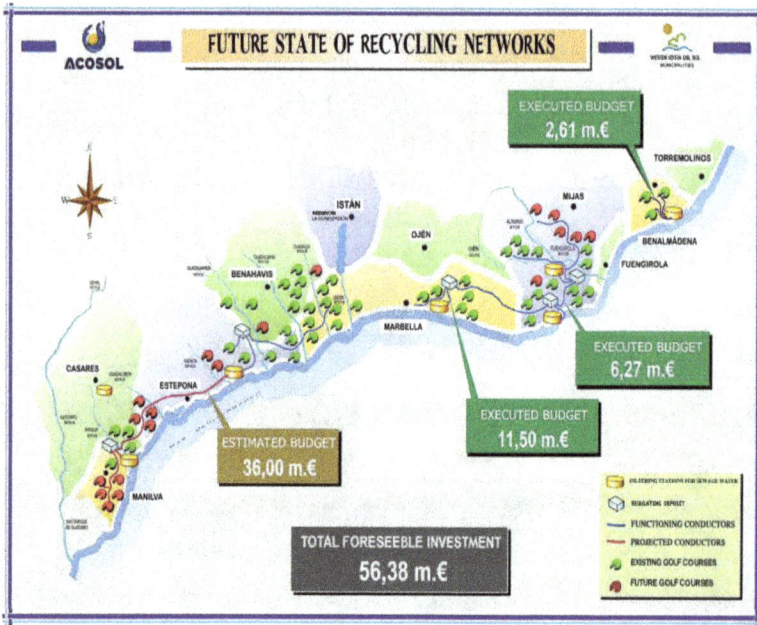

CHART III: FUTURE STATES OF PURIFYING SYSTEMS

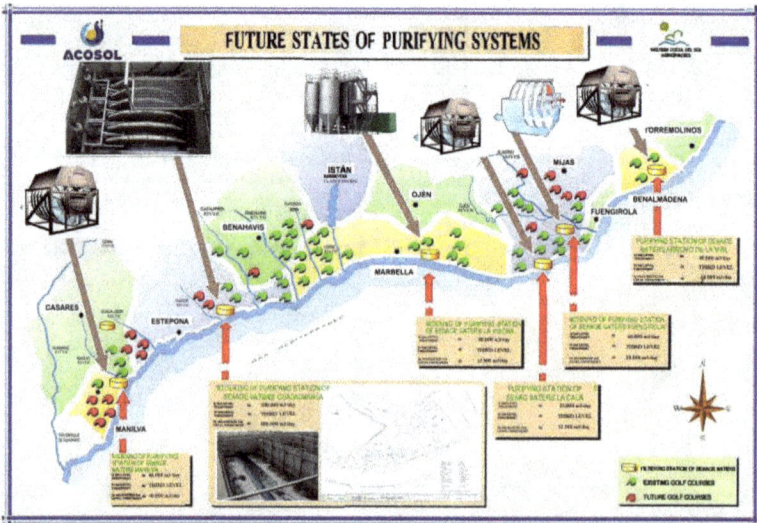

CHART IV: INTEGRATION OF GOLF COURSES INTO
THE RECYCLING SYSTEM

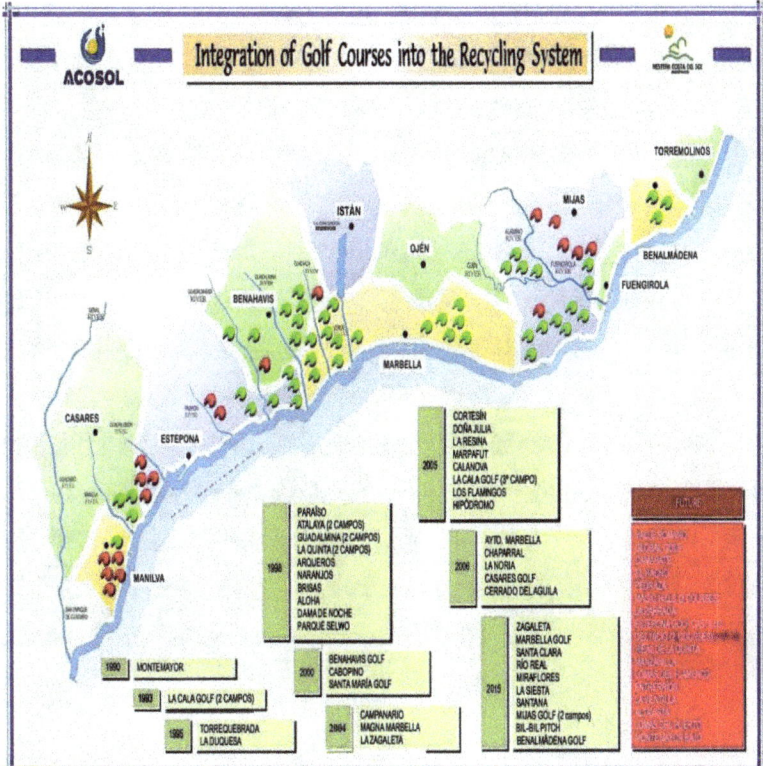

CHART V: MONTHLY RAINFALL l/m²

VOLUME IN RESERVOIRS Hm³

MONTH / YEAR	JANUARY	FEBRUARY	MARCH	APRIL	MAY	JUNE	JULY	AUGUST	SEPTEMBER	OCTOBER	NOVEMBER	DECEMBER	ANNUAL AVERAGE
1989	38,310	58,719	59,299	58,947	56,667	52,260	45,942	39,458	34,686	36,757	52,089	51,729	48,739
1990	54,765	56,293	61,433	61,475	61,122	57,848	52,013	45,205	39,543	34,908	34,819	39,441	49,907
1991	38,564	46,264	59,941	60,604	58,408	54,081	47,934	40,707	34,790	36,977	34,775	37,264	45,859
1992	35,617	40,370	42,581	46,207	42,497	38,796	34,729	28,260	22,698	28,742	17,907	15,782	32,257
1993	14,135	21,214	25,102	24,656	25,065	22,456	18,567	14,004	10,781	9,794	30,336	31,563	20,640
1994	33,132	33,649	34,936	33,428	30,898	26,510	20,764	14,388	9,772	7,650	7,260	6,007	21,533
1995	5,528	5,149	4,414	3,458	2,593	1,568	0,882	0,500	0,472	0,528	1,139	21,962	4,016
1996	55,182	58,826	60,153	60,670	61,630	60,953	57,646	53,399	50,875	48,750	50,287	54,063	56,020
1997	54,105	59,584	60,932	60,574	59,352	57,351	53,019	48,219	46,549	46,587	52,024	52,943	54,352
1998	56,024	55,055	59,100	59,015	58,510	55,961	51,710	46,682	43,037	39,847	37,148	36,150	49,853
1999	37,399	37,601	41,653	42,784	42,733	40,100	34,966	29,322	25,078	27,623	27,853	28,288	34,608
2000	44,320	49,528	49,899	56,993	59,963	58,678	54,689	49,737	44,792	41,248	39,965	56,020	50,469
2001	57,141	56,804	57,309	57,751	56,003	51,881	45,695	38,935	34,493	32,688	38,412	56,467	48,832
2002	57,704	58,468	60,217	61,702	60,279	56,445	50,571	43,071	37,534	33,857	36,786	49,205	50,496
2003	58,025	59,016	61,340	60,764	60,427	56,635	50,249	42,328	35,913	43,763	56,804	53,626	53,308
2004	55,982	55,350	57,288	59,500	59,142	55,814	49,680	42,902	37,196	33,620	30,173	31,416	47,339
2005	28,672	26,357	35,869	34,759	31,208	25,986	19,259	12,227	7,155	5,409	5,556	6,922	19,948
2006	16,213	28,208	51,539	57,309	57,267	54,651	49,680	43,543	38,851	36,608	52,051	54,347	45,829
2007	55,413	58,341	58,131	58,784	57,141	52,488	46,701	40,539	36,682	34,729	32,904	42,058	47,833
2008	48,389	53,988	57,583	60,363	59,247	55,392	49,471	42,682	40,339	40,994	52,507	54,803	51,328
2009	54,480	57,240	58,173	57,141	53,911	49,376	43,560	36,771	31,623	27,968	25,423	54,908	45,882
2010	54,727	56,382	61,684	61,648	61,467	57,941	51,843	44,708	39,593	35,528	34,360	56,845	51,227
2011	54,158	57,120	62,226	60,932	61,908	59,837	54,866	49,110	44,252	42,328	53,683	53,531	54,496
2012	52,621	50,951	48,960	46,321	44,202	39,810	34,128	27,904	24,055	26,062	55,889	94,992	42,128
2013	56,698	56,656	58,341	62,014	61,594	58,994	53,455	47,403	42,750	39,087	35,454	33,368	50,485
2014	32,658	39,711	39,357	40,657	34,429	34,729	28,467	22,082	18,775	17,542	33,975	43,577	32,163
2015	47,744	50,306	58,046	59,015	56,382	52,280	46,094	39,982	35,617	35,218	39,104	37,720	46,459
2016	36,994	37,753	37,720	39,441	57,983	55,708	50,780	43,948	38,209	34,789	40,404	54,708	44,036
2017	55,308	57,077	59,805	59,774	58,763	54,651	49,395	43,948	37,956	34,729	33,102	31,771	48,007

CHART VI: COMPARATIVE IRRIGATION RAINY/DRY YEAR

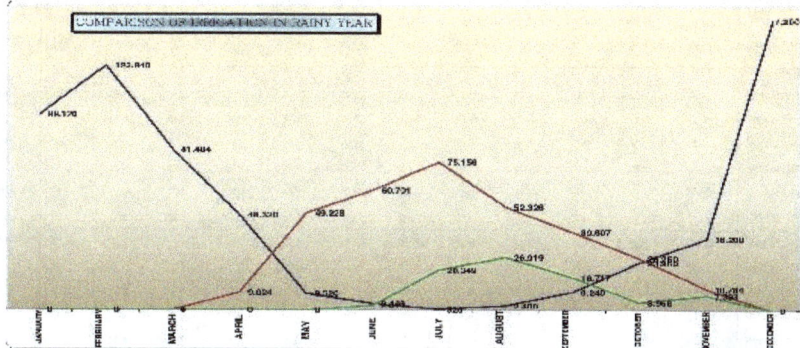

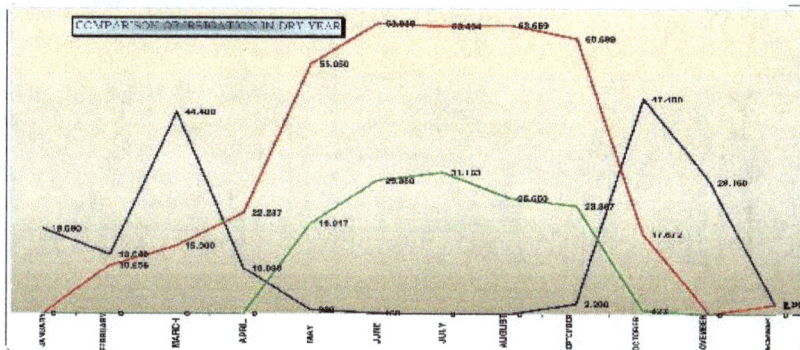

CHART VII: HYDRAULIC YEAR CHART l/m^2

HYDRAULIC YEAR l/m^2

ACOSOL

	OCTOBER	NOVEMBER	DECEMBER	JANUARY	FEBRUARY	MARCH	APRIL	MAY	JUNE	JULY	AUGUST	SEPTEMBER	TOTAL HYDRAULIC YEAR
From 2000 to 2001	61,65	84,70	283,70	115,60	35,80	117,80	0,00	67,00	0,00	3,10	0,30	81,00	850,65
From 2001 to 2002	67,90	70,60	151,55	26,30	8,40	103,00	65,20	6,30	0,70	0,00	0,00	21,00	520,95
From 2002 to 2003	64,10	183,20	141,30	47,20	89,40	87,75	93,45	0,60	0,30	0,00	0,00	0,00	707,30
From 2003 to 2004	253,85	84,00	194,30	7,90	139,65	123,10	44,30	24,10	0,00	10,40	0,00	0,00	881,60
From 2004 to 2005	81,70	2,15	116,70	3,20	63,70	116,50	12,30	10,30	0,00	0,00	0,00	2,00	408,55
From 2005 to 2006	55,10	47,70	47,00	174,10	65,20	126,30	38,30	5,40	13,40	2,10	14,70	5,90	595,20
From 2006 to 2007	82,60	188,60	22,60	53,40	61,20	13,00	70,40	39,80	0,10	0,50	1,50	91,80	625,50
From 2007 to 2008	47,10	34,00	174,60	44,20	80,40	36,40	108,20	33,10	0,40	0,00	0,00	182,00	740,40
From 2008 to 2009	71,40	191,60	77,70	43,80	152,90	37,20	25,90	4,50	1,10	0,00	0,00	13,40	619,50
From 2009 to 2010	19,70	31,90	454,20	247,80	309,60	203,51	120,80	21,30	8,60	0,80	6,00	23,10	1.447,31
From 2010 to 2011	89,90	90,50	368,00	105,00	41,10	176,40	100,70	70,30	6,90	0,00	0,50	0,40	1.019,70
From 2011 to 2012	157,10	170,40	0,50	40,00	6,70	12,00	59,10	27,70	0,00	0,80	0,00	40,30	524,60
From 2012 to 2013	139,50	267,90	36,30	28,00	152,70	222,70	51,70	6,20	0,00	0,00	0,00	31,20	936,20
From 2013 to 2014	25,20	1,80	53,20	50,80	74,00	14,00	67,60	14,90	2,70	0,00	0,00	35,20	339,20
From 2014 to 2015	74,20	224,80	24,30	46,70	32,60	111,20	25,20	2,30	0,40	0,00	0,00	5,50	547,20
From 2015 to 2016	118,70	72,90	5,90	36,90	24,10	22,20	44,50	91,60	0,00	0,00	0,00	1,90	418,70
From 2016 to 2017	45,20	154,30	293,80	14,60	89,70	74,70	84,10	0,00	0,00	0,00	2,00	2,00	760,50

CHART VIII: HYDRAULIC YEAR GRAPH l/m^2

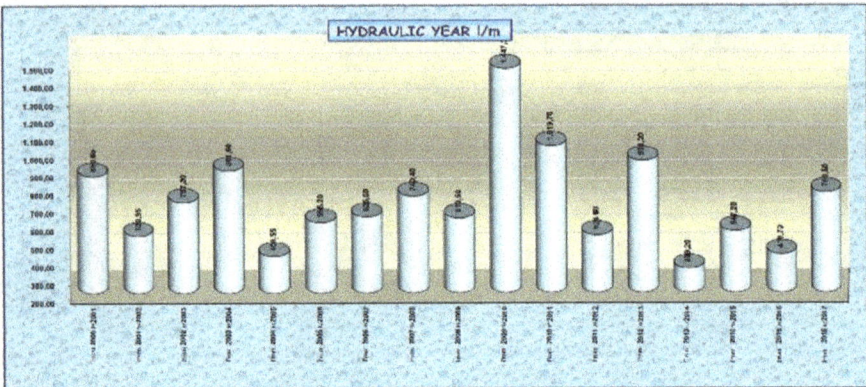

HYDRAULIC YEAR l/m

Maps

MAP I: POLITICAL MAP OF COSTA DEL SOL

MAP II: ANNUAL PRECIPITATION MAP OF THE IBERIAN PENNINSULA

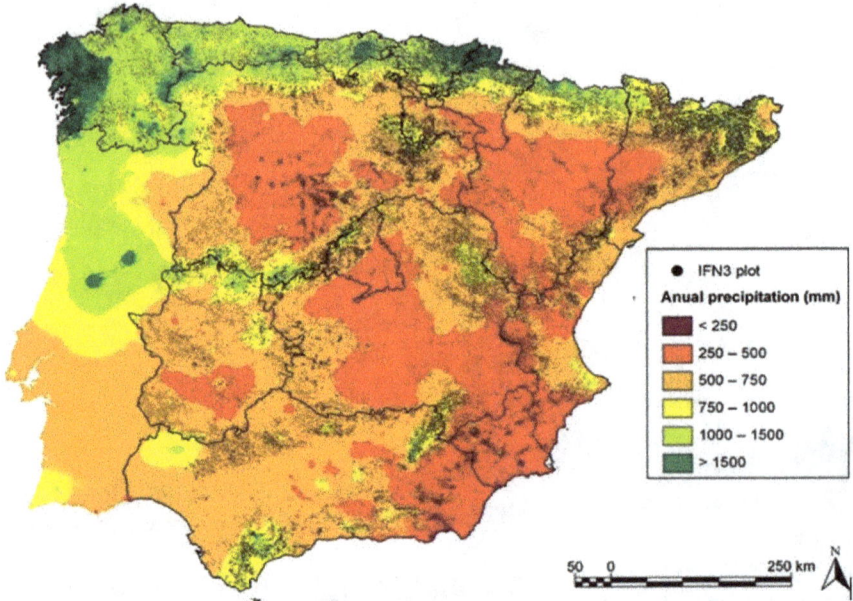

MAP III: The Town of Torremolinos and the System of Roads

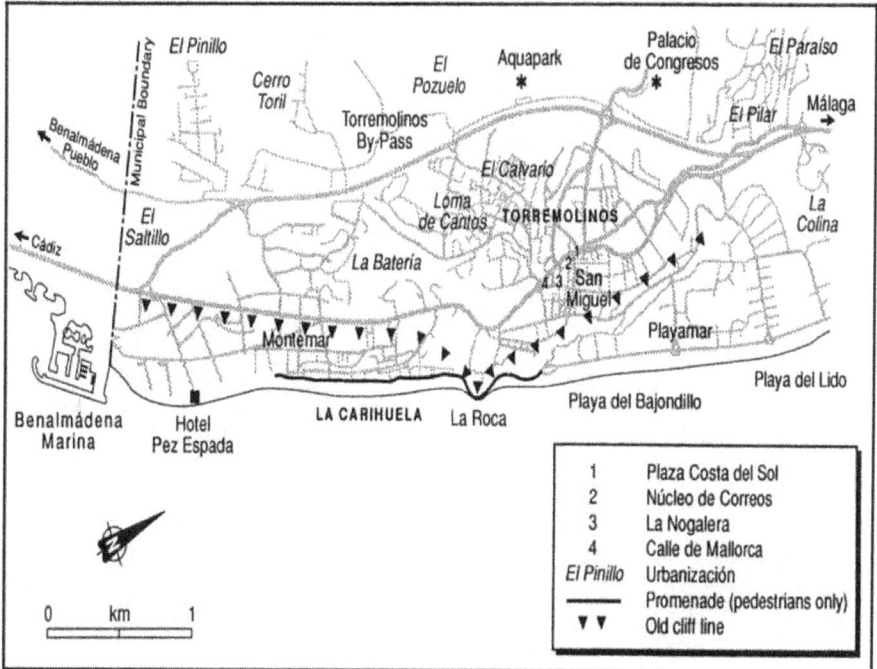

1	Plaza Costa del Sol
2	Núcleo de Correos
3	La Nogalera
4	Calle de Mallorca
El Pinillo	Urbanización
———	Promenade (pedestrians only)
▼ ▼	Old cliff line

Sources: J. Pollardy, R. Domínguez Rodríguez, 1995.

BIBLIOGRAPHY

Agarwal, Sheela. *Coastal Resort Restructuring and the TALC.* Vol. 2, in *The Tourism Area Life Cycle. Conceptual and Theoretical Issues.*, by Richard W. Butler, 201-230. Clevedon: Channel View Publications, 2006.

———. "Restructuring Seaside Tourism: The Resort Lifecycle." *Annals of Tourism Research* 29, no. 1 (2002): 25-55.

———. "The Geography of Tourism Production: Uneven Disciplinary Development?" *Tourism Geogprahies* 3, no. 3 (2000): 241-263.

Akerhielm, Peter, Chekitan S. Dev, and Malcolm A. Noden. "Europe 1992: Neglecting the Tourism Opportunity." *The Cornell Hotel and Restaurant Administration Quarterly*, 1990: 104-111.

Alteljevic, I., and S. Doorne. "Staying Within the Fence: Lifestyle Entrepreneurship in Tourism." *Journal of Sustainable Tourism* 8, no. 5 (2000): 378-392.

Ambientum. "Riego de campos de golf." *Revista Ambientum*, January 2004.

Andronicou, A. "Tourism in Cyprus." In *Tourism: Passport to Development*, edited by de Kadt, 237-264. Oxford: Oxford Univeristy Press, 1979.

Arenas Gómez , Andrés , and Jesús Majada Neila. *Viajeros y turistas en la Costa del Sol: (de Rilke a Brenan).* Málaga: Miramar, 2003.

Baedeker, Karl. *Spain and Portugal: Handbook for Travellers.* Leipzig: Baedeker Publishers, 1908.

Bao, J., and C. Zhang. *The Tale in China's Tourism Planning: Case Study of Danxia Mountain, Guangdong Providence, PRC.* Vol. 1, in *Aspects of Tourism, The Tourism Area Life Cycle, Applications, and Modifications*, by Ricahrd W. Butler, edited by Richard W. Butler, 107-116. Clevedon: Channel View Publications, 2006.

Barke, M, J. Towner, and Michael Newton. "Exploring the History of Leisure and Tourism in Spain." In *Tourism in Spain: Critical Issues*, edited by M. Barke, J. Towner and M. Newton, 3-34. Wallingford: CAB International, 1996.

Barke, M., and L. France. "The Costa del Sol." In *Tourism in Spain: Critical Issues*, by John Towner, Michael Barke, and Michael T. Newton, edited by Michael Barke, John Towner and Michael T. Newton, 265-308. Wallingford: CAB International, 1996.

Barnes, Trevor J. "Retheorizing Economic Geography: from the Quantitaive Revolution to the 'Cultural Turn.'" *nnals of the Association of American Geographers* 91, no. 3 (2001): 546-565.

Bejarano, José. "El monstruo insaciable de la Costa del Sol." *La Vanguardia*, 2005.

Bishop, Paul L. *Marine Pollution, and Control.* London: McGraw Hill, 1983.

Blouet, Brian W. *The EU & Neighbors: A Geography of Europe in the Modern World.* Hoboken: John Wiley & Sons, 2007.

Boissevian, J., and P. Inglott. "Tourism in Malta." In *Tourism: Passport to Development?*, edited by E. de Kadt, 265-284. Oxford: Oxford University Press, 1979.

Boniface, Brian, Robyn Cooper, and Chris Cooper. *Worldwide Destinations: The Geography of Travel and Tourism.* 6. Vol. 1. Amsterdam: Elsevier Butterworth-Heinemann, 2005.

Briguglio, L., and L. Vella. "The Competitiveness on the Maltese Islands in the Mediterranean International Tourism." In *Island Tourism: Management Principals and Practice*, edited by M. Conlin and T. Baum, 133-147. London: Wiley, 1995.

Brougham, J.E., and Richard W. Butler. "The Applicability of the Asymptotic to the Forecastimg of Tourism Development." *Presentation at the Research Workshop, Travel Research Association.* Quebec, July 1972.

Bull, Adrian. *The Economics of Travel and Tourism.* Melbourne: Pitman Publishing, 1991.

Bunge, William. "Modeling Tourism Development: Evolution, Growth and Decline." In *Tourism, Development and Growth*, by S. Wahat and J. John, edited by Piyram, 109-125. London: Routledge, 1997.

———. *The concept of a Tourist Area Cycle of Evolution: Implications for Management of Resources.* Vol. 1, in *Aspects of Tourism. The Tourism Area Life Cycle, Applications and Modifications*, edited by Richard W. Butler, 13-25. Clevedon: Channel View Publications, 2006a.

———. *The Origins of the Tourism Area Life Cycle.* Vol. 1, in *Aspects of Tourism. The Tourism Area Life Cycle Applications and Modifications*, edited by Richard W. Butler, 13-26. Clevedon: Channel View Publications, 2006b.

———. *Theoretical Geography.* London: C.W.K. Gleerup Publishers, 1966.

Butler, Richard. *The London Times*, 2006: 6.

———. "Modelling Tourism Development. Evolution, Growth and Decline." In *Tourism, Development, and Growth*, by S. Wahat and J. John, edited by S. Wahat and J. John, 109-122. London & New York: Routledge, 1997.

———. *The Tourism Area Life Cycle, Vol. 2, Conceptual and Theoretical Issues by Richard W. Butler.* Vol. 2. Clevedon: Channel View Publications, 2006.

——— *Pre- and Post-Impact Assessment of Tourism Development. Tourism Research: Critiques and Challenges.* New York: Routledge, 1993.

———. "The Concept of a Tourist Area Cycle of Evolution: Implications for Management of Resources." *Canadian Geographer* 24, no. 1 (1980): 5-12.

———. *The Tourism Area Life Cycle (Vol. 1: Applications and Modifications).* Vol. I. Cleveland: Channel View Publications, 2004.

Butler, Richard W., and J.E. Brougham. "The Applicability of the Asymptotic Curve to the Forecasting of Tourism Development." *Travel Research Associate 4th Annual Conference.* Quebec, July 1972.

Carrington, R. *The Story of Our Earth.* New York: Harper & Row, 1956.

Christaller, W. "Beitrage zu einer Geographie der Fremdenverkehr." *Erdkunde*, February 1955.

Closa, Carlos, and Paul M. Heywood. *Spain and the European Union.* New York: Palgrave, 2004.

Cooper, Chris. *The Anatomy of the Rejuvenation Stage of the TALC.* Vol. 2, in *The Tourism Area Life Cycle, Conceptual and Theoretical Issues*, edited by Richard W. Butler, 183-200. Clevedon: Channel View Publications, 2006.

Corak, Sandra. "The Modification of the Tourism Area Life Cycle Model for (Re)inventing a Destination: The Case of the Opatija Riviera, Croatia." In *The Tourism Area Life Cycle Vol. 1: Applications and Modifications*, edited by Richard W. Butler, 271-286. Clevedon: Channel View Publications, 2006.

Costa, P., and M. Manente. "Venice and its Visitors: A Survey and a Model of Qualitative Choice." *Journal of Travel and Tourism Marketing* 4, no. 3 (1995): 45-69.

Crawford-Welch, Simon, and Eliza Tse. "Mergers, Acquisitions and Alliances in the European Hospitality Industry." *International Business Communication* 4, no. 3 (1990): 42-48.

Dahles, Heidi. "Redefining Amsterdam as a Tourist Destination." *Annals of Tourism Research* 25, no. 1 (1998): 55-69.

Danta, Dr. Derek, interview by Pamela L. Perez. *Late Dean of School of Social and Behavioral Sciences, California State University, Northridge* (October 2007).

De Albuquerque, Klaus, and Jerome L. McElroy. "Caribbean Small-Island Tourism Styles and Sustainable Strategies." *Environmental Management* 5, no. 16 (1992): 619-632.

Debbage, Keith. "Tourist Destination Cycles and Sustainable Development: A Comparative Analysis of the Bahamas and Mauritius." *Annals of Tourism Research* 17 (1990): 513-527.

———. "Air Transportation and International Tourism: The Regulatory and Infrastructural Constraints of Aviation Bilaterals and Airport Landing Slots." In *Reflections on International Tourism: Management, Marketing and the Political Economy of Travel and Tourism*, edited by M. Robinson and et al., 67-83. Gateshead: Business Education Publishers, Ltd., 2000.

Dicken, Peter. *Global Shift: Transforming the World Economy.* London: Sage, 2004.

Digance, Justine. "Life Cycle Model." *Annals of Tourism Research* 24, no. 2 (1997): 152-154.

Diputacion de Malaga. *El Turismo Residencial y de Segunda Residencia en la Provincia de Málaga.* Málaga: Sociedad de Planificación y Desarollo, 2007.

Douglas, Ngaire. "Applying the Life Cycle Model to Melanesia." *Annals of Tourism Research* 24, no. 1 (1997): 1-22.

Florida, Richard. *The Rise of the Creative Class*. New York: Basic Books, 2002.

Foster, Danny, and Peter Murphy. "Resort Cycle Revisited: The Retirement Connection." *Annals of Tourism Research* 18, no. 4 (1991): 553-567.

Gatt, J. *Decline in Tourism - Causes and Effects, Doctoral Dissertation*. Malta: Univeristy of Malta, 1984.

Gay, Kathlyn. *Pollution and the Powerless: The Environmental Justice Movement*. New York: Franklin Watts, 1994.

Getz, Donald. "Tourism Planning and Destination Life Cycle." *Annals of Tourism* 4, no. 19 (1992): 752-770.

Godkin, Edwin Lawrence. "The Nation." In *The Tourism Area Life Cycle Applications and Modifications*, by Richard W. Butler, 13-26. Clevedon: Channel View Publications, 1883.

Goodall, B. "Understanding Holiday Choice." In *Progress in Tourism, Recreation and Hospitality Management*, edited by Chris Cooper, 58-77. London: Belhaven, n.d.

Grennon, Michael, and Michel Batisse. *Futures for the Mediterranean Basin: The Blue Plan*. Oxford: Oxford University Press, 1989.

Guillén, Mauro. *The Rise of Spanish Multinationals: European Business in the Global Economy*. Cambridge: Cambridge University Press, 2005.

Haywood, K. Michael. "Evolution of Tourism Areas and the Tourism Industry." In *spects of Tourism, The Tourism Area Life Cycle, Applications and Modifications*, edited by Richard W. Butler, 51-69. Clevedon: Channel View Publications, 2006.

Haywood, M.K. "Can the Tourist Area Life Cycle be Made Operational?" *Tourism Management* 7, no. 3 (1988): 154-167.

Hobbs, Conrad. "The Origins of the Tourism Area Life Cycle." *Worcester Magazine*, September 14, 1915: 13-26.

Holguin, Sandie. "National Spain Invites You: Battlefield Tourism During the Spanish Civil War." *American Historical Review* 110, no. 5 (2005): 1399-1426.

Hovinen, Gary. *Lancaster County, the TALC, and the Search for Sustainable Tourism*. Vol. 1, in *The Tourism Area Life Cycle Vol. 1, Applications and Modifications*, edited by Richard W. Butler, 73-90. Clevedon: Channel View Publications, 2006.

Ioannides, Dimitri. "Commentary: The Economic Geography of the Tourist Industry: Ten Years of Progress in Research and an Agenda for the Future." *Tourism Geographies* 8, no. 8 (February 2006): 76-86.

———. "Tourism Development Agents: The Cypriot Resort Cycle." *Annals of Tourism Research* 19, no. 4 (1992): 711-731.

Johnston, Charles Samuel. "Shoring the Foundations of the Destination Life Cycle Model, Part 1: Ontological and Epistemological Considerations." *Tourism Geographies* (Taylor & Francis Ltd.), 2001: 2-28.

Jurado Arrones, F. *España en Venta*. Madrid: Ediciones Endimión, 1999.

Jurado, Enrique N. *¿Puede seguir creciendo la Costa del Sol? Indicdores de saturación de un destino turístico.* . Málaga: CEDEMA, 2003.

Kigance, J. "Life Cycle Model." *Annals of Tourism Research* 24, no. 2 (April 1997): 152-155.

King, R., and et al. "Editorial Introduction." *International Journal of Population Geography*, no. 4 (1998): 87-89.

Kirby, S. J. "Recreation and Quality of Spanish Coastal Waters." In *Tourism in Spain: Critical Issues*, by John Towner, Michael Barke and Michael T. Newton, edited by John Towner, Michael Barke and Michael T. Newton, 189-211. Wallingford: CAB International, 1996.

Kousis, Maria. "Tourism and the Family in a Rural Cretan Community." *Annals of Tourism Research* 16 (1989): 318-332.

Kulikowski, Michael. *Late Roman Spain and its Cities*. Baltimore: John Hopkins Univeristy Press, 2004.

Kunstler, James Howard. *The Geography of Nowhere: The Rise and Decline of America's Man-Made Landscape*. New York: Simon & Schuster, 1993.

Lagiewski, Rich. "The Application of the TALC Model: A Literature Survey." In *Aspects of Tourism, the Tourism Area Life Cycle, Applications and Modifications*, edited by Richard W. Butler, 27-50. Clevedon: Channel View Publications, 2006.

Lardies, Raúl. "Migration and Tourism Entrepreneurship: North-European Immigrants in Cataluña and Languedoc." *International Journal of Population Geography*, 1999: 477-491.

Libreri, J. *Foreign Settlers in Malta: An Economic Analysis, Doctoral Dissertation.* Malta: Univeristy of Malta, 1971.

Lichorish, L. "European Tourism 1992 – The Internal Market." *Tourism Management* 10, no. 2 (1989): 100-110.

Lockhart, D. "Tourism to Malta and Cyprus." In *Island Tourism Trends and Prospects*, edited by D Drakakis-Smith, 152-178. London & New York: Pinter, 1997.

López López, Alejandro. *El Espacio Ambiental Europeo. Edición de la Universidad Complutense de Madrid y del Instituto Nacional de Consumo.* Madrid, 1990.

———. "Desarrollo Sostenible: Medioambiente y turismo en las ciudades históricas: El caso de Toledo." *Observatorio Medioambiental* 8 (2005): 331-344.

———. "El medio ambiente y las nuevas tendencias turísticas: referencia a la región de Extremadura." *Observatorio Medio Ambiental* 4 (2001): 205-251.

———. "Requisitos medioambientales para un programa de acción sobre Turismo Rural en la Comunidad Autónoma de Madrid." *Observatorio Medioambiental*, no. 7 (2008): 195-222.

———. "Turismo y Medioambiente." *Tribuna Complutense*, May 24, 2008: 24.

———. "Turismo y Medio Ambiente en España." *El Espacio Ambiental Europeo. Edición de la Universidad Complutense de Madrid y del Instituto Nacional de Consumo*, 1990: 121-137.

———. "Turismo y Desarollo Sostenible." *Sistema*, June 2001: 162-163, 189-202.

———. "Turismo, medio ambiente y desarollo en el horizonte de 1992 las provincias de Guadalajara y Teruel." *El Espacio Ambiental Europeo*, 1990: 139-156.

———. "Otra mirada turismo y medioambiente." *La contra, tribuna Complutense*, May 24, 2005: 24.

López López, Alejandro, and Javier De Esteban Curiel. "Turismo , internet e indicadores ambientales de sostenibilidad." *Observatorio Medioambiental* 11 (2008): 185-199.

Marchena Gomez, Manuel. "Los impactos particulares del turismo en Andalucía: la configuración especial y demográfico-social de San Pedro de Alcántara." *Estudios Regionales*, no. 20 (1998): 89-108.

———. "Sobre politica regional del turismo en Andalucía." In *Desarollo regional y crisis del turismo en Andalucía. Actas del Simposio Hispano-Frances*, edited by Andres Garcia Lorca and Francis Fourneau, 339-389. 1991.

Marois, J., and T. Hinch. *Seeking Sustainable Tourism in Northern Thailand: The Dynamics of the TALC.* Vol. 1, in *The Tourism Area Life Cycle, Vol. 1, Applications and Modifications*, edited by Richard W. Butler, 250-268. Clevedon: Channel View Publications, 2006.

Martin, B. "The TALC Model and Politics." In *he Tourism Area Life Cycle, Vol.1 Applications and Modifications*, edited by Richard W. Butler, 237-249. Clevedon: Channel View Publications, 2006.

Martin, B. S., and M. Uysal. "An Examination of the Relationship Between Carrying Capacity and the Tourism Area Lifecycle: Management and Policy Implications." *Journal of Environmental Management* 31, no. 7 (1990): 327-333.

McDowell, Joanne, R.W.G. Carter, and H. John Pollar. "The Impact of Man on the Shoreline Environment of the Costa del Sol, Southern Spain." In *Tourism vs Environment: The Case for Coastal Areas*, edited by P.P. Wong, 189-209. Dordrecht: Kluwer Academic Publishers, 1993.

Mead, William Edward. *The Grand Tour in the Eighteenth Century.* New York: Houghton Mifflin, 1914.

Meyer-Arendt, Klaus J. "The Grand Isle, Louisiana Resort Cycle." *Annals of Tourism Research* 12, no. 3 (1985): 449-465.

Mihalik, Brian J. "Tourism Impacts Related to EC 92: A Look Ahead." *Journal of Travel Research* 32, no. 4 (1991): 27-32.

Morris, Arthur. "Environmental Management in Coastal Spain." In *Tourism in Spain: Critical Issues*, edited by M. Barke and et al., 213-228. Wallingford: CAB International, 1996.

Morris, Arthur, and Gordon Dickinson. "Tourist Development in Spain: Growth versus Conservation on the Costa Brava." *Geography* 72, no. 288 (1987): 16-25.

Munoz, P., and E. Miranda. "Evolution and Problems of Recycled Water in Western Costa del Sol." *The International Conference on Golf and the Environment.* Roqueta: ACOSOL, Public Limitied Company, 2007.

Noble, John, Isabella Noble, Lonely Planet, Josephine Quintero, and Brendan Sainsbury. *Andalucía.* London: Lonely Planet, 2004.

Norhona, R. *Social and Cultural Dimensions of Tourism: A Review of the Literature in English.* Washington D.C.: World Bank Working Paper, 1977.

O'Reilly, Karen. *The British on the Costa del Sol: Transnational Identities and Local Communities.* London: Routledge, 2000.

Pack, Sasha. *Tourism and Dictatorship: Europe's Peaceful Invasion of Franco's Spain.* New York: Palgrave Macmillan, 2006.

Pais, El. "Campos sin urbanizaciones y regados." *El Pais,* August 8, 2006.

Pearce, David, and Kerry Turner. *Economía de los Recursos Naturales del Medio Ambiente.* Madrid: Colegio de Economistas de Madrid y Celeste Ediciones, 1995.

Pisani, C. *An Economic Assessment of the Construction Industry and Recent Property Boom, Doctoral Dissertation.* Malta: University of Malta, 1972.

Pollard, John, and Rafael Domínguez Rodríguez. "Unconstrained Growth: The Development of a Spanish Resort." *Geography* 80, no. 346 (January 1995): 33-44.

Prats Palazuelo, F. "SOS en el litoral español." *Ciudades para un futuro más sostenible.* Madrid, July 1-5 2005.

Priestley, Gerda, and Lluis Mundet. "The Post-Stagnation Phase of the Resort Cycle." *Annals of Tourism Research* 25, no. 1 (1998): 85-111.

Punds, N. *Europe and the Mediterranean.* New York: McGraw-Hill , 1953.

Relations, U.S. Congress House Committee on International. "Subcommittee on Travel and Tourism Partnership Act: Joint Hearing Before International Economic Policy and Trade." Washington: House of Representatives, One Hundred Fourth Congress, n.d.

Resort, La Cala. "La Cala Resort Newsletter." Summer 2007, 26.

Rodríguez Martínez, Francisco. "El impacto ambiental del turismo." In *Desarollo regional y crisis del turismoen Andalucía, Actas del Simposio Hispano-Francés,* edited by Andrés y Francis Fourneau Lorca, 331-388. 1991.

Rodríguez, Vicente, Fermina Rojo-Pérez, and Gloria Fernandez-Mayoralas. "European Retirees on the Costa Del Sol: A Cross-National Comparison." *International Journal of Population Geography,* no. 4 (1998): 183-200.

Rosendorf, Neal Moses. "Be El Caudillo's Guest: The Franco Regime's Quest for Rehabilitation and Dollars after World War II via the Promotion of U.S. Tourism to Spain." *Diplomatic History* 30, no. 3 (2006): 367-407.

Ruiz Aviles, P., et al. "El turismo rural en Andalucía ante la reforma de la PAC." In *Desarollo regional y crisis del turismo en Andalucía. Actas del Simposio Hispano-Francés.,* edited by García Lorca, Andrés and Francis Fourneau , 133-144. 1991.

Russell, Roslyn, and Bill Faulkner. "Movers and Shakers: Chaos Makers in Tourism Development." *Tourism Management* 20, no. 4 (August 1999): 411-423.

Russo, Antonio P, and Jan van der Borg. "Planning Consideration for Cultural Tourism: A Case Study of Four European Cities." *Tourism Management* 5, no. 23 (2002): 165-182.

Russo, Antonio P. "A Re-foundation of the TALC for Heritage Cities." In *Aspects of Tourism. The Tourism Area Life Cycle, Applications and Modifications,* edited by Richard W. Butler, 139-161. Clevedon: Channel View Publications, 2006.

Shelby, Byron, and Thomas Heberlein. *Carrying Capacity in Recreation Settings.* Corvallis: Oregon State University Press, 1986.

Shields, Rob. *Lifestyle Shopping: The Subject of Consumption.* London: Routledge, 1992.

Stannard, Dorothy. *Insight Guides: Southern Spain: Costa del Sol – Andalicía.* 4a. Basingstoke: Geocenter International, Ltd., 2006.

Stansfield, Charles A., and John E. Rickert. "The Recreational Business District." *Journal of Leisure Research* II, no. 4 (1970): 20.

Strapp, James D. "The Resort Cycle and Second Homes." *Annals of Tourism Research* 15, no. 4 (1988): 504-516.

Tooman, L. Alex. "Applications of the Life-Cycle Model in Tourism." *Annals of Tourism Research* 1, no. 24 (1997): 214-234.

Towse, R. "Venice as a Supeesrstar." *Paper presented at the Conference of Economies of the Cities of Art.* Venice, May 13-15, 1991.

Tremlett, Giles. *Ghosts of Spain: Travels Through Spain and its Silent Past.* New York: Walker and Companhy, 2007.

Truemann-Watkins, B. "Phoenicians in Spain." *Biblical Archaeologist* 55, no. 1 (1995): 29-34.

Tsartas, Paris. "Socioeconomic Impacts of Tourism on Two Greek Isles." *Annals of Tourism Research* 19, no. 6 (1992): 516-533.

Urry, John. *The Tourist Gaze: Leisure and Travel in Contemporary Societies.* London: Sage, 1990.

van den Berg, L., and E. Braun. "Urban Competitiveness, Marketing, and the Need for Organizing Capacity." *Urban Studies* 36 (1999): 987-999.

Water Recycling and Reuse: The Environmental Benefits. n.d. http://www.epa.gov/region09/water/recycling/ (accessed April 8, 2007).

Weatherly, R. *Tourism and Rural Development: The Mountain Districts of Andalusia Spain, Ph.D. Thesis.* Vol. I and II. Keele: University of Keele, 1981.

Wheeler, Brian. *The King is Dead, Long Live the Product: Authenticity, Sustainability, and the Product Life Cycle.* Vol. 1, in *The Tourism Area Lifecycle, Vol. 1, Applications and Modifications*, edited by Richard W. Butler, 339-347. Clevedon: Channel View Publications, 2006.